THE DAVID HUME INSTITUTE 1991

THE MORALITY OF BUSINESS ENTERPRISE

THE DAVID HUME INSTITUTE

THE MORALITY OF BUSINESS ENTERPRISE

Norman Barry

ABERDEEN UNIVERSITY PRESS
Member of Maxwell Macmillan Publishing Corporation

First published 1991
Aberdeen University Press

© The David Hume Institute 1991

British Library Cataloguing in Publication Data

Barry, Norman
  The morality of business enterprise. — (David
  Hume paper series)
  I. Title II. Series
  174.4

ISBN 0 08 037964 8

Printed in Great Britain at BPCC-AUP Aberdeen Ltd

Foreword

To David Hume, the inspirer of this Institute, the transformation of an economy from a predominantly agricultural state to one in which manufacturing flourished had produced a refinement in human behaviour and temper. Following Hume, nineteenth century writers extolled the commercial order as a great moral achievement. In doing so, they contrasted the peaceful development of trade between nations, which rested on mutual trust and honesty, with the baser ambitions and behaviour associated with the pursuit of war.

In essence, Professor Barry's monograph follows this classical tradition but in an era when there is a marked hostility towards its general thesis. Even if it is accepted that in the business and financial world there must be 'rules of the game', the critics of the business and financial world are convinced that its activities lure its members into morally hazardous situations which are detrimental to society. In consequence, they argue that the rules need drastic revision and this could mean imposing regulations on business enterprises which go beyond those imposed on other sections of society. This conventional wisdom has extended its influence as a result of some quite sensational business scandals associated with stock exchange operations and corporate takeovers.

As Professor Barry shows, appraising business behaviour with a view to establishing a 'workable' system of business ethics is a much more difficult task than appears at first sight. It calls for a thorough understanding of the operation of the market economy and the claims made for it. As he shows, much of the moral criticism is based on a false conception as to how markets work. Further, as he argues: 'the difficult and interesting problems of business ethics arise because there is usually a plurality of principles at work in the evaluation of commercial activity'. Those seeking a fuller understanding of business ethics must therefore brace themselves for a closely argued account of the nature of ethical systems. In short, this monograph provides the reader with an introduction to moral philosophy but cleverly applied to a subject of great contemporary interest.

Having warned the reader that he is expected to work hard, I hasten to emphasise that it would be difficult to find a better qualified guide through the maze of specious arguments and emotional outpourings on business practice. That is not to say that Profesor Barry is an uncritical admirer of business practices. This is evident in his fascinating analysis of the moral

v

dilemmas encountered in those corporate actions which have attracted the public's interest.

It must always be made clear that the Institute has no collective view on public policy issues. At the same time, the Institute is glad to have this opportunity of publishing what it regards as a major contribution, one which complements the Institute's recent report on corporate takeovers* prepared for the Joseph Rowntree Foundation.

* See Alan Peacock and Graham Bannock, *Corporate Takeovers and the Public Interest*, Aberdeen University Press for The David Hume Institute, 1991.

Contents

Preface

In this short book I have attempted to outline in general, and to explore in more detail in some instances, a view of the morality of business enterprise in Western capitalist democracies. In some respects my approach is a little unconventional since it runs counter to much of the received tradition in American business ethics. From its beginning as a serious academic subject this tradition has extended the notion of business morality beyond the observance of conventional legal and moral rules into more contentious social issues so that a range of moral duties has been imposed on business that has little connection with commerce. It seems to me that there are enough difficulties for business in the following of ordinary moral rules without entering into the contentious realm of social issues. Many of the prescriptions that are addressed to it derive from disputed social and political philosophies rather than from manageable business ethics.

I have also on occasion questioned the genuine morality of much of expanded business ethics. Since many writers stress the fact that it is in the interests of business to behave in a 'socially responsible' fashion one is entitled to doubt that these motives would be regarded as genuinely moral by traditional ethical philosophers. Many people regard particular actions as morally right quite irrespective of the good consequences that they might bring to agents. In fact, as I suggest, the ideal of a competitive economy, which has undeniably certain moral as well as efficiency qualities, leaves little room for the kind of social duties that many business ethicists would impose on commercial agents. I also suggest that under conditions of competitive markets, the rule of law and a not undemanding level of consumer autonomy at least some of the familiar problems of business ethics are 'filtered out', i.e. solved without the need for a legislated business ethics. However, I have pointed to clear examples of business behaving in unethical ways by the standards of ordinary morality. The lure of profit is, and always will be, a powerful distraction from moral duty. Bernard Mandeville's famous distinction, in *The Fable of the Bees*, between commerce and virtue (that we cannot expect to be both prosperous and moral) is too strong. As a clever and amusing diversion it is perhaps best applicable to those extended notions of morality which, if 'enforced', would indeed make commerce impossible. Still, for all his cynicism, Mandeville did point to a serious problem.

I have concentrated on the moral issues that arise in the context of the large-scale corporation, those that emerge in the stock market and in the struggle for corporate control (takeovers). It is in these areas that spectacular business scandals have occurred in the last ten years. I have said very little about business and the environment. This is likely to be the big issue for the next decade and I have deferred discussion of it until a future occasion. However, I have indicated what I think is the appropriate framework for such an analysis.

The bulk of the research for this book was pursued while I was Visiting Scholar at the Social Philosophy and Policy Center, Bowling Green State University, Ohio, for the year 1989–90. I am extremely grateful to the Directors of the Center for providing excellent research facilities and a congenial atmosphere for study. I am also indebted to the Wincott Foundation for its grant in support of the research and to Professor Sir Alan Peacock of the David Hume Institute, Edinburgh; especially for his tolerance of my dilatoriness in completing the manuscript.

Last, but by no means least, I would like to thank my secretary at Buckingham, Mrs Anne Miller. Not only did she type innumerable drafts but she was indispensable in the gathering and organising of much of the original research materials (including making a translation from French).

Norman Barry
Buckingham
May 1991

Acknowledgement

The Trustees of the David Hume Institute are deeply grateful to the Wincott Foundation for the offer of financial support towards the preparation of this publication.

for Luana

1   Ethical Value Systems and Business

Why Business Ethics?

Business ethics as an academic discipline is a comparative newcomer to the typical university curriculum, and geographically limited to the United States: though, of course, the ethics of business, the morality of capitalism, the profit motive and the justice (or injustice) of free markets have been topics explored repeatedly since the beginnings of the commercial civilisation in eighteenth-century Europe. Capitalism itself may be said, not inaccurately, to have a morally tainted biography in that its mainsprings tend to derive from the baser human motives, self-interest and the desire for personal profit. Its success, to many people, seems to depend on the suspension, if not outright rejection, of those moral constraints on individual gratification that are said to be integral to Western morality. Furthermore, the cultivation of some of the traditional moral virtues, honesty, integrity, self-sacrifice and the charitable instinct, seems to be hampered, if not made impossible, by the competitive impulse which is the driving force of the enterprise of business. Many people would regard the peroration in favour of 'greed' (a motivation to be cultivated to the exclusion of conventional moral imperatives) delivered by the Wall Street arbitrageur, Ivan Boesky, to a group of business students in 1986, as only a slightly hyperbolic description of the egoistic psychology and amoral attitudes that drive the business community. Boesky said that: 'Greed is all right by the way. I want you to know that. I think greed is healthy. You can be greedy and still feel good about yourself.'[1]

Indeed, many of the well-publicised scandals of recent years, 'insider dealing' in the stock market (for which Boesky was eventually convicted), bribery in the pursuit of lucrative contracts, despoliation of the environment in the desire for profit and many other venalities allegedly perpetuated by business, lend a superficial credence to the popular view of capitalism. Even in America, although capitalism itself is not regarded as morally condemnable, the activities of business corporations and their senior employees are regarded with some cynicism by the public at large and even more so by the intellectual community.[2] Religious groups especially have sedulously stressed the anti-social and amoral (if not immoral) nature of business. Even the spokesmen of business have done little to question what is sometimes known as the 'myth of amoral business'.

The 'ethics' of competition have, at least since the end of the nineteenth century, been regarded as no more than Social Darwinism, a social application of the biological doctrine of the 'survival of the fittest', in which it is 'right' that inefficient firms, organisations and individuals should be sacrificed in the relentless and remorseless competitive process. To impose social duties on business enterprises and individual entrepreneurs, either by coercive law or by conventional morality, would be to weaken competition and place arbitrary obstacles in the way of progress. Despite philosophical objections to the assimilation of the 'good' to whatever has emerged through competition, the doctrine that business is self-justifying has historically not been unimportant. It was given a superficial moral gloss by the attribution of indefeasible moral rights to individuals, so that, irrespective of the question of social progress, government action that violated an individual's right to exchange, to enjoy the products of his own labour and to accumulate wealth were in principle condemnable. This idea was as much a part of Herbert Spencer's social philosophy as his doctrine of evolution (indeed, the two ideals—rights and social progress—were claimed to be harmonious) and it is echoed in some *laissez-faire* arguments today.

For most of the twentieth century little was done to counter this contaminated image of capitalism, an image cultivated by intellectuals. In fact, capitalism was attacked on two fronts. One argument, from orthodox Marxists, claimed that, irrespective of its moral failings, capitalism and the market were destined for extinction by inexorable social 'laws': competition between firms would drive down the rate of profit causing industry to be concentrated in a few hands, increasing mechanisation would create a revolutionary 'reserve army' of the unemployed and the succession of booms and slumps of an undirected market would eventuate in a final 'crisis' from which socialism (and ultimately communism) would emerge triumphant. The manifest failure of socialist planning and the recent rush into market arrangements in formerly communist regimes in Eastern Europe, however, has not so much validated the morality of capitalism as decisively negated the utopianism of collectivist planning: capitalism may not be 'just' but it works. Thus the second, and now more fashionable critique of capitalism, centres almost entirely on its moral failings. Business ethics as a discipline is very much concerned to evaluate capitalist enterprise by reference to morality.

The recognition of the efficiency of capitalism, of course, has a long and honourable history in the writings of political economists, but even from this perspective the credit accorded to it was provisional: the efficiency ethic had to be supplemented by an external morality if it were to be acceptable. Thus when business ethics began to be taken seriously in the US, at the beginning of the 1960s, the dominant *motif* of the writers was that commerce had to be restrained by an appeal to justice, rights, social utility and other concepts drawn from the traditional Western moral vocabulary. Thus firms were urged to serve the community and not just the stockholders; to refrain from activities which, although lawful, might have an adverse effect on society at large; to honour justice by adopting hiring policies which, although technically inefficient, favoured deprived minorities; to refrain from bribery in international dealings even though that might be an accepted practice in the countries with which they are involved; to be honest in advertising, and so on. The emphasis was mainly on the corporation, an institution to which was attributed social and moral duties as well as strictly economic ones. The 'social audit' was held to be as important as the financial one.[3]

Of particular importance was the moral status of the corporation itself. The animus against business (both in the US and Britain) was not so much against enterprise, but against 'Big Business': the giant corporation (to be considered in detail below), with its legal privileges of limited liability, perpetual life, separation between management and owners, and so on, was itself held to be a threat to the (not unacceptable) market order. Its alleged power to exempt itself from competition, to collude and fix prices and exploit individuals, to harm communities through morally arbitrary plant relocations and to attenuate market disciplines through its dealing with government, became the target of intellectuals, such as John Kenneth Galbraith[4] and political activists, such as Ralph Nader.[5]

In fact, if anything the defence (what little there was) of capitalist behaviour since the Second World War has taken a rather different form from one which might identify it as a special kind of virtue. This defence represents commerce and business as somehow separate from morality (although of course not outside the rules of civil and criminal law): that it was simply inappropriate to impose upon participants moral duties that are distinct from the conventional ethical rules that apply to everyone as citizens. Thus to expect businessmen and corporate executives to display virtue by going beyond what the law requires in the way of fair employment practices or protection of the environment, would be to disrupt the genuine rules of business relationships, most notably the contractual arrangement between the management of a corporation and its stockholders. Indeed, its most articulate spokesman, Milton Friedman, claims that the attribution of social responsibilities to businessmen, if successful, would allow them to arrogate political functions.[6] The assimilation of special virtues to business enterprise would also, Friedman claims, lead to the attenuation of the property rights of the owners of corporations (i.e. the shareholders). However, many critics have mistakenly interpreted this view to mean that business is outside the realm of ordinary morality, that virtue and commerce do not mix, and that the phrase 'business ethics' is an oxymoron.

The 'Myth of Amoral Business' perhaps originates in the infamous *Fable of the Bees*[7] by the eighteenth century writer, Bernard Mandeville. In his parable, Mandeville posited a dichotomy between virtue and commerce, that the adoption of traditional Christian standards of self-restraint and charity makes everyone worse off, as well as running counter to the universal mainsprings of human action. The encouragement of the baser motives would lead to an extension of the division of labour, the widening of the market and the growth of international trade, all of which would make everyone better off. But this encouragement, he claimed, could not make us virtuous. Hence his observation of the bee-hive in its *non-moral* state: 'Every part was full of vice / Yet the whole mass an earthly paradise'.

This attitude perhaps does not quite eliminate morality from business, since the whole activity is given an overall utilitarian justification; however, the application of 'Mandevillianism' to capitalism seems to confirm the argument that successful business requires a suspension of at least some virtues. Contemporary business ethicists are, in effect, either validating Mandeville's argument by suggesting that capitalism and virtue are not naturally compatible so that ethical standards have to be imposed on businessmen by the artifice of law, or trying to refute him with the argument that ethics is, in fact, 'good for business', i.e. moral restraint is ultimately profitable. Of course, the cynic might suggest that even the latter view is a subtle manifestation of the Mandevillian spirit, since it sees the observation of moral rules as instrumentally rather than intrinsically valuable.

It is doubtful, however, whether even the most extreme opponents of the 'social responsibility of business' thesis are really Mandevillians. After all, the rigid dichotomy between virtue and commerce would permit certain business practices, such as bribery (itself a complex issue), yet the most vociferous free market advocates contend that business must not only be conducted within the law but also be consistent with general morality. Milton Friedman, for example, claims that, although the only responsibility of business is to maximise profits, this activity must be pursued in conformity to the 'basic rules of the society, both those embodied in law and those embodied in ethical custom'.[8] The problem is to determine what the customary ethical rules are and what they imply for the practice of business. A generous interpretation of them would narrow the gap between the proponents of business freedom and its critics. At least, it is doubtful whether any would claim that business need necessarily be 'amoral'. What is important here is a distinction between the attribution of normal moral responsibility to business agents and the imposition of *additional* social duties. Whilst the distinction is clear enough in theory, in practice there may well be serious problems.

In fact, what is probably behind the case for free markets is a much older argument; that commerce has positive moral advantages even apart from the utilitarian considerations that might tell in its favour. It is the claim that the business relationship, so far from being destructive of moral values, actually advances them; that peaceable co-operation and exchange between individuals in search of gain improves their character. This was certainly the argument of the eighteenth- and nineteenth century celebrants of commercial society, Montesquieu, David Hume, Adam Smith (with some qualifications) and Benjamin Constant.[9] Of course, the virtues of the market seemed obvious enough to these writers, since the contrast that they drew was between trade and war; self-glorification through markets was more enlightened morally than national glory through global conflict. In their eyes, the very anonymity of market society, with its opening up of the possibility of peaceful relationships between strangers held together only by simple rules and the cash nexus, was itself a moral achievement. In the nineteenth century, of course, global conflict between nations as a contrast to peaceable exchanges was replaced by conflict between classes. It is no accident that Herbert Spencer, in lamenting the decline of the commercial order, complained that its replacement by socialism was not a progressive move but a recrudescence of an older, 'militant' form of society.

It is perhaps regrettable that historically this aspect of the justification for business proved to be short-lived, vulnerable as it was to Marxist historicism and to the more overtly moral criticism of commerce: the latter was directed more at the emergence of industrial and corporate forms of business society than the simple commercial order described by Adam Smith. However, contemporary apologists for capitalism are implicitly drawing upon this tradition when they contrast the market and the state; the former being the realm of spontaneous co-ordination of otherwise disparate individuals while the latter is often depicted as a coercive institution for the imposition of plans upon individuals. Indeed, the corporation itself is seen by some writers[10] as having a moral purpose, forming a locus of identity for individuals who would otherwise be either soulless inhabitants of an anonymous market or subservient to an all-powerful state (as in communist regimes). The moral value of the 'personality' of the corporation then holds independently of the overtly utilitarian value of this form of economic organisation.

The contrast between the state as an instrument of coercion and the market as a realm of co-operation has proved very useful to writers favourable to the idea that business *itself* can solve some of the familiar problems of modern economies. The damage to the environment that unrestrained industrial activity can produce, the necessity for rules to govern trading in the securities market and the desirability of certain sorts of hiring practices are all problems which can be treated without departing from the traditional and valuable concept of economic man as co-operative man. If businessmen were to get together, as Kenneth Arrow[11] suggests, and devise rules themselves to enforce moral standards in the above areas, this co-operation might be criticised as just another example of self-interest, i.e. their actions would be motivated by the desire to avoid more harmful state intervention, but it need not necessarily be interpreted as immoral. For one thing it would illustrate the fecundity of the explanatory artifice of 'economic man'; it would reveal that it is not limited to the description of how self-interested actions can lead to market co-ordination but can be extended to show how individuals can co-operate under general rules when it is not in their immediate interest so to do. For another, such spontaneous co-operation would indicate that the psychological motivation of capitalism is not amoral or socially destructive, even in the least propitious of circumstances. It would be a manifestation of the Enlightenment spirit rather than the cynical attitude of Bernard Mandeville.

All this suggests that throughout its history commercial activity has been to a limited extent a moral enterprise: an activity that required the recognition of constraints on human action and the submission of individuals to rules of just conduct be they explicit, as in the criminal and civil law, or tacit, as in the 'rules of the game' that have traditionally governed financial and asset markets. Business is historically a part of Western civilisation yet it is that part which has failed to receive the approbation of the moralists of the twentieth century. The virtues of the commercial age looked real enough to Adam Smith when contrasted with the bellicosity of former times but in the contemporary world business has been set more exacting tasks by the whole panoply of moral philosophy, including the promotion of social justice, equality, rights and the public interest.

It has been hampered mainly by the fact that the traditional business values seem to be at odds with some of the dominant themes of contemporary social philosophy. Conformity to rules and procedures seems to be too minimal an ethic to sustain the values of the business enterprise: such minimalism might permit actions which, although lawful, run counter to current moral standards. Since these standards have included, from the end of the last war at least, a commitment to social or redistributive justice, the enterprise society has been especially vulnerable. The allocative mechanisms of the market necessarily involve inequality of factor reward, and this phenomenon bears only the faintest resemblance to conventional distributive criteria, such as desert or need. Thus the fact that Michael Milken earned $550 million in 1987 on Wall Street was as decisive in the moral condemnation of him as the wrongs or harmful acts for which he was eventually prosecuted. It seems to be the conventional wisdom that a person cannot earn that kind of money without harming someone (though economic theory would have it otherwise).

The Difficulties of Self-Restraint

The possibility of business regulating itself in the way that other professions, such as law and medicine, have through established and enforced codes of ethics independently of governments, seems remote. This is so, despite the fact that, as suggested above, it would be in the business community's self-interest to do so. The reason is that such co-operative activity comes up against a familiar problem in social theory—the 'public good' trap (or, in the technical literature, the 'Prisoner's Dilemma').[12] Put simply, this means that co-operative activity, which would be to the benefit of rational, self-interested agents, is unlikely to be forthcoming through the voluntary action of the same agents, since however well motivated each person might be he cannot be sure that the others will be so reliable. In the absence of well-defined property rights, for example, individuals will exploit land and natural resources for their own immediate advantage, even though such activity often harms everyone.

The existence of this phenomenon creates real dilemmas for business. A familiar example is the problem of pollution. The business community has been assailed by ethicists for not taking account of the environment in its profit-maximising activities: the 'moral audit' would include therefore the costs imposed on third parties. Yet pollution cannot be wholly bad, for the activity that generates it is productive of jobs and lower prices for consumers. It cannot be assumed that the efficiency solutions produced by the state produce an appropriate balance between, on the one hand, productivity, employment and lower costs, and on the other, environmental protection.

An example is the current Clean Air Act recently passed by the American Congress. It is conceded that this will impose heavy costs on industry, costs that will ultimately be passed on to the public in the form of higher prices, fewer jobs (temporarily) and lower returns to stockholders. What cannot be known is whether the gains the community secures in the way of environmental protection exceed the costs measured in orthodox business terms. Many observers think that they will not but, however that may be, it is unlikely that the business community could behave with the kind of self-restraint which is required for it to resist such legislation.

Again, it is improbable that the self-enforced 'rules of the game' in the financial world would have been sufficient to restrain those practices, insider dealing, the fixing of share prices and so on, which seem to be an affront to widely held conceptions of justice. The result has been, in the US especially, excessive regulation which has in fact hampered the efficiency of these markets and, as we shall see below, brought threats to the rule of law. In Britain, even with the Financial Services Act of 1986, the City of London is to some extent self-regulating. However, the code of ethics under which it operates is regarded as inadequate by critics who recommend that it should be replaced by something akin to the more coercive American model. The omnipresence of self-interest in business makes it appear morally feeble and hence vulnerable to intervention.

It is not my argument to show that such interventions are efficient, or even 'right' by the tenets of contemporary business ethics—indeed, in America, a great deal of individual injustice has been done by a sometimes over-zealous Securities and Exchange Commission—but only to suggest that the nature of business activity in the modern world makes it peculiarly ill-equipped to resist such encroachment. Even if business were not 'amoral', the structure of a complex, anonymous market society makes it difficult for the participants to honour even those conventional ethical standards which business ethics would impose on them. This is largely because business agents find themselves in dilemmas: problems to which our pluralistic moral systems produce radically different answers.

The Meaning of the Market

The reason why the business community has been subjected to moral criticism, the explanation of its vulnerability to extra-economic ethical imperatives, derives partly from the fact that the environment in which it necessarily operates, the market, does not, and never has, operated in the way that the textbook models describe. I shall show later that a large part of the business ethics school misunderstands the market and that much of the criticism of capitalism emanates from this misunderstanding, but it is important to indicate at this stage the source of the criticism. It is that 'imperfect' markets generate those opportunities for business to behave in a way that is seen to be morally reprehensible by its critics.

As it is depicted in micro-economics texts, the ideal of a perfectly competitive market has certain features which make it possible for it to be used as an ethical standard (even though it is normally used in a quasi-scientific way). In a world of many firms, none of which can influence price, where there is costless entry, an absence of externalities and perfect information on the part of all participants, some of the problems of business ethics would be definitionally absent. For example, perfect information would preclude the possibility of insider dealers in securities taking an 'unfair' advantage of other people's ignorance, competition would have whittled factor earnings down to the minimum required for efficient production so that there would be no entrepreneurial 'profit', and the ability of free agents to make highly specific employment contracts would exclude those problems of 'civil rights' and 'authority' in the workplace which arise from the highly general contracts that are made in the modern business enterprise.

Of course, none of this is meant to imply that there cannot be legitimate moral criticisms of competitive markets even if they tended to work in the way the textbooks describe. The psychological foundation upon which they rest may be said to be not a universal attribute of man but a contingent feature of a pre-existing set of capitalist institutions; the theory says nothing about initial resource endowments, which may be condemnable from the perspective of social justice; 'welfare' is limited to the satisfaction of individual desires when there may be other actions that may be plausibly advanced as welfare-enhancing; and the market, by treating individuals as anonymous maximisers, separates them from their communal bonds and attenuates the altruistic sentiment. These, and many other, objections have been raised against even well-functioning markets.

However, the intuitive appeal of the 'idea' of the market is now great enough to attract socialists formerly wedded to central planning. This is no doubt due to the market's freedom-enhancing properties and, surprisingly, to the fact that its distributive mechanisms seem often to produce results that are broadly (though by no means entirely) consistent with widely held notions of the just reward (though it was not the intention of the founders of the theory to claim this harmony between payments to factors and desert[13]). It is the way in which capitalist economies have developed that has provoked the need for business ethics rather than the idea of exchange itself.

It is crucial to stress that it is the presence of the corporation that generates the problems adumbrated above; and it is the rationale of this institution and the ethical justification for some of its behaviour that are relevant to the moral evaluation of business enterprises. For the corporation or the firm (I shall use these terms interchangeably except where the context requires them to be distinguished) is absent from the classical model of perfect competition and it was scarcely present in the 'virtuous' commerce of the late eighteenth century described by the early apologists of market capitalism. It is its great power, and perhaps more importantly, that of its management, and its (alleged) relative immunity to market processes, to moral and political con- straint that have generated most of the problems located by business ethicists. It should be apparent that the defender of business enterprise, and its attend- ant culture, cannot make simple appeals to the ideals of perfectly competitive markets alluded to above. For one thing, not only have they never obtained in practice but a variant of them, the commercial society and its attendant virtue described by early writers is no longer with us. The presence of the large corporation or conglomerate in the contemporary world has made a moral difference. For another, the world of perfect competition is very much the ideal of market socialism;[14] and this means the defender of capitalism has not only to show that the 'perfect' competition model is an inadequate explanation of the way that markets work, but also that the phenomena that it excludes, especially profit, are not only functionally necessary but ethically desirable (or, at least, not condemnable).

The Ambit of Business Ethics

The ethics of business encompass two major areas: they may be termed the macro and the micro. The macro is about the validation of the enterprise culture, especially in its corporate manifestation. This involves such questions as the nature and justification of the market and the role of profit within it, the 'social responsibility' or otherwise of business, the regulation of commerce and the rule of law. The micro issues are about ethical problems that arise in the day-to-day activities of the business corporation and private agents. Should ethical constraints be allowed to override profit-maximisation in plant relocation? Does the employment contract deprive the employee of his 'rights' to criticise the firm publicly ('whistle-blowing')? Does insider dealing necessitate unfairness in the securities market? Is a corporation under a moral duty to go beyond legal requirements in order to aid disadvantaged minorities?

The principles that are used in the evaluation of business activity are likely to be the same whether they are used in macro- or micro level problems. Thus an ethicist who regards the market and the profit system as justifiable on utilitarian grounds is likely to be highly sceptical of restraints on business activity, for example, the imposition of wide social obligations on business corporations: they are condemned as destructive of market mechanisms. On the other hand, a sceptic of these mechanisms would welcome such restraints as necessary consequences of the application of morally superior principles of social organisation. Thus, if the doctrine of justice implies that there should be a 'level playing field' for business activity, then the enforcement of insider trading rules in the stock market is legitimate, even if such a policy, as some theorists maintain, coagulates the flow of information on which the successful co-ordination of activities depends.

However, the difficult and interesting problems of business ethics arise because there is usually a plurality of principles at work in the evaluation of commercial activity. Few apologists for business would claim that restraint on its actions should be limited to that provided by the law; indeed the idea of commerce as a civilising influence would be incoherent in the absence of certain ethical conventions. Again, few writers on the Left, apart from unreconstructed opponents of capitalism and the market order, maintain a complete indifference to the effect on productivity that the rigorous commitment to abstract moral principles might have.

In fact, most moralists pay an unwitting tribute to the commercial ethic by arguing that morality is 'good business'. This might be the case in the aggregate but surely the problems arise precisely in those situations where morality is costly for a particular enterprise, and where, for reasons alluded to above, individual corporate agents cannot be expected (or predicted) to shoulder the burdens imposed by the necessity of maintaining a morality that favours that aggregate but not themselves taken individually. There is no escaping that business dilemmas largely arise out of the competing claims made on agents by utility, justice, the environment, rights and, indeed, the whole range of morality. However, all this requires an understanding of the meaning, and substantive implications, of these ethical concepts.

What Ethics for Business?

In ethical theory there are, to simplify matters, two competing approaches to the evaluation of conduct, whether it is the behaviour of politicians, ordinary people in their daily lives, or business (either the appraisal of the whole system or actions by individual agents operating under its rules): they are the *teleological* and the *deontological*.[15] These apparently irreconcilable value systems colour, in one form or other, all of our moral judgements. Briefly, teleological judgements are based upon some desirable state of affairs, either for an individual or a group, which some action brings about: and the action is evaluated in accordance with its conduciveness to this state of affairs. It is states of affairs themselves that are intrinsically valuable rather than the actions that bring them about. Deontological principles relate to those moral duties that restrain us from performing certain actions irrespective of the value of consequences. The duties themselves are intrinsically compelling. This perhaps crude dichotomy conceals a host of complexities and subtleties but it, nevertheless, encapsulates well enough the ethical context within which business is conducted. Nevertheless, I shall show later that it is a somewhat misleading view of business ethics to see it as a simple application of one or the other of these moral philosophies to particular problems. The practice of business, like any other social activity, generates rules which are not easily described in the conventional language of moral philosophy. Business ethics, like the ethics of ordinary life, is too complex to be captured by one all-embracing theory.

The teleological theory most relevant here is utilitarianism: that ethical doctrine which evaluates states of affairs in terms of happiness, welfare, well-being or some other phenomenon that relates to identifiable satisfactions.[16] There are teleological doctrines that locate intrinsic value in other things than sensuous experience, for example, self-realisation or some Aristotelian notion of virtue, but they make only fleeting appearance in the literature of business ethics, even though they are frequently significant.

Deontological doctrines are best represented by justice: there are certain moral rules of fairness which are so compelling that our adherence to them overrides all other considerations; they are necessary side-constraints on action. Although utilitarians always try to incorporate the rules of justice (fair dealing, giving each person his due, the obligatory nature of promises, and so on) into a comprehensive moral calculus by arguing that they are conducive to overall utility, it is not difficult to see how conflicts can arise between the demands of justice and the dictates of utility. Perhaps it is immoral to trade with South Africa because it is an unjust regime: but if it can be shown, as surely it can, that everyone is made worse off (the blacks suffering most of all) by a ban or by voluntary acts of restraint, then these prohibitions themselves would be immoral by the criterion of utility. In contrast, the deontologist discounts consequences (although it is a rare theorist who discounts them entirely) in his evaluations and therefore he will have good reasons for condemning such trade.

It should be clear from the above example that utilitarianism is not the only ethics relevant to business activity, that commerce is not merely to be evaluated in terms of a calculus of pleasures and pains. Yet it is superficially its most plausible rationale. Since commerce is an activity that responds to people's wants and desires it seems the ideal candidate for favourable evaluation by a moral doctrine that exclusively understands good and bad in terms of want-satisfaction. However, utilitarianism is itself a complex doctrine, the meaning of which is constantly in dispute, and the prescriptions of which are not always determinate.

It bears a superficial similarity to the Mandevillian doctrine mentioned earlier: that business does not rest upon virtue but self-interest and that the latter motivation is validated morally (if at all) by the fact that it generates beneficial outcomes. Although there is more than a trace of Mandevillianism in 'Invisible Hand' versions of utilitarianism, Mandevillianism itself has not secured a respectable niche in business ethics: utilitarianism proper, however, has. It is a comprehensive ethical doctrine and (unlike the 'amoral business' view) has implications at the micro level of business activity which can and do run counter to the egoism and amoralism implied in *The Fable of the Bees*. Business may be said to generate practical rules which, although they may have an ultimate utilitarian justification, are inconsistent with, and could condemn, egoism. The rules for the self-regulation of business activities would be of this type.

Utilitarianism supposes that actions are to be evaluated solely in terms of how much they contribute to the well-being or happiness of a community: rules, conventions and orthodox moral principles have a provisional value only, and are subordinate to the compelling imperative to maximise happiness. In the work of the doctrine's founders, notably Jeremy Bentham (1748–1832), happiness could be calibrated in discrete units of pleasure, the pursuit of which, it was alleged, was the sole purpose of human endeavour. Pleasure was assumed to be as tangible as heat and cold, and a 'hedonic' calculus was proposed for evaluating actions which would be as accurate in the measurement of pleasure as a thermometer is for recording temperature. Two further assumptions are made by Benthamite utilitarians: every person is the best judge of his own interest, and every person's interests must be taken into account in the overall calculation of utility. The former requirement rules out paternalism and the latter is a vague and ambiguous commitment to a notion of equality of consideration. It should be noted that there is only a contingent (though some would say, easily demonstrable) connection between the maximisation of social utility and the existence of the private enterprise, commercial order.

Because of the difficulty of measuring pleasure, and making interpersonal comparisons of utility, contemporary economists tend to limit their welfare judgements to that implied in the 'Pareto principle': this holds that it is only possible to speak of a welfare improvement when an action (e.g. a two-person exchange) makes (at least) one person better off without making anybody else worse off.[17] Although it rests on a similar view of human motivation to utilitarianism, it is in theory much weaker. Since it precludes inter-personal comparisons of utilities it must remain silent on actions that although generally beneficial, harm at least one person, however minutely.

Because of the requirement to take everyone's interests into account, and to perform intricate (and some would say, impossible) calculations as to the social effects of alternative courses of action, utilitarianism imposes controversial and almost always conflicting duties upon agents. Thus a utilitarian-minded management of a corporation would, in plant relocation decisions, have to take into account the interests of a community whose residents had 'invested' in the firm, the interests of the shareholders who would benefit from efficiency, those in another community who might be badly in need of employment, and so on. These are extraordinarily difficult calculations; great enough, critics of 'business ethics' would say, to negate the very possibility of a 'social audit' for business derived from utilitarian considerations alone.

Unfortunately, the Pareto principle is not much help in such problems either. Operating on a restricted notion of harm, a Paretian could maintain that untrammelled markets, in the absence of externalities, do maximise social welfare in the sense described. But the operation of market forces, generating never-ending change and uncertainty, leaves many people who can claim to be 'harmed'. The Pareto principle is too weak ethically to give any firm guidance in this vexed area. It has little use in the texts of business ethics: except perhaps at the macro level, in the overall justification of the market system. At the micro level, in the justification of particular business decisions, harm itself appears to be a contestable concept.

Despite the problems inherent in the notion of pleasure, and the insuperable difficulties of aggregation, the major elements of utilitarianism have survived. Whether it is pleasure that ought to be maximised, or the superficially more tractable notion of preferences, it is always to the consequences of action to which moral appeal is made, and the restraints imposed by moral and conventional rules are acceptable only if they are conducive to good outcomes, however these are understood. Utilitarianism does not necessarily justify the capitalist system: indeed, it might well validate constant interventions in search of improvements in cases where suffering might appear to be avoidable. Such a superficially benign doctrine, one exclusively addressed to human well-being and unencumbered by possibly archaic rules, has not surprisingly appealed to governments and the owners and managers of business enterprises. Business agents who wish to act ethically constantly make rough and ready comparisons between the gainers and losers of alternative policies.

However, it bristles with problems, both at the macro and micro level of appraisal. In a world of flux and certainty, how can it be known what the consequences of a policy or action are? How are we to evaluate short-term and long-term consequences? How far should the interests of future generations be taken into account (a point most pertinent to the problems involved in business and the environment)? Does not the fact that moral principles and conventional rules are regarded as provisional only, to be discarded if by so doing some benefit can be secured, offend against our moral sense? The last point is most important; for in the absence of an objective way of measuring utility, arbitrariness can surely occur with the application of the utilitarian judgement. The injunction that 'all interests be taken into account' operates as a minor restraint only. Taking people's interests into account does not necessarily imply that everybody will be treated fairly, or guarantee that the ensuing calculation of overall utility will not offend against our intuitive moral principles.

Utilitarian considerations are sometimes present in decision-making in business when cost-benefit analysis is used. It is especially relevant in product safety. A corporation will often take a controversial decision on the basis of a measure of the benefits of the product, taking into account the interests of consumers, stockholders and employees, compared to the costs of safety requirements. Safety considerations alone cannot be decisive, it is claimed, since no product can be perfectly safe and utility gains will be foregone because of the probably excessive costs involved in the pursuit of an unattainable ideal of a perfectly harmless product. Often the costs of potential litigation in civil actions will be included in the final calculations, and it is this factor that can make corporations vulnerable to the charge of cynicism.

A spectacular example of this cynicism was the notorious Ford Pinto case in the US in the late 1970s.[18] The Ford Motor Corporation was anxious to market a new car and it knew that its model had a design fault: the petrol tank was likely to explode after a collision at the rear. The costs of correcting it would have badly affected Ford's market prospects so the company went ahead with the original product after taking into account the costs of civil damages if an accident were to occur. All the above utilitarian considerations were relevant to the decisions. However, Ford's action could be said to be condemnable on both utilitarian and deontological grounds. From a consequentialist point of view, the interests of all affected parties were not equally considered and from a deontological perspective, people (i.e. customers) were not treated as ends in themselves but as mere counters in a cost-benefit calculation.

In fact, serious collisions did occur which led to the deaths of many people. However, Ford's calculations misfired, since the corporation was eventually prosecuted for the *criminal* offence of 'reckless homicide'. The latter generated another problem (to be considered below) for business ethics: whether it is legitimate for a legal fiction, such as a public corporation, to be criminally liable for actions which only biological persons can be said to be capable of performing.

An instructive example of a genuine clash between utilitarian considerations and abstract (deontological) moral principles occurred in the marketing in the Third World by Nestlé of a product ('infant formula') which was used by mothers instead of breast-feeding their babies.[19] This was known to have unfortunate side-effects if it were misused (especially if the formula was diluted with contaminated water). This did, indeed, occur and there were some deaths through ill-informed mothers failing to use the product correctly. Despite the mounting adverse evidence, Nestlé continued an aggressive marketing strategy, and defended its policy on straightforward utilitarian grounds. Nestlé claimed that the benefits far outweighed the costs and, furthermore, argued that it could not be held responsible for the misuse of its product. This last point is particularly instructive since it invites the question as to whether the utilitarian maxim that 'everyone knows their own interests best' is always applicable in the product market, especially in under-developed countries where education, and living standards in general, are low.

Many examples could be produced to show that in private business matters, tensions between utilitarian considerations and moral principles involving justice, right and duties and so on, occur in exactly the same way as they do at the macro level. It is for this reason that utilitarianism is sometimes reformulated in such a way as to accommodate the binding nature of moral and conventional rules. The above examples were cases of *act-utilitarianism*: the claim here is that agents should always act so as to produce the greatest possible benefit on every occasion and that his conduct should be guided by this rather than the dictates of a rule.

However, *rule-utilitarians*[20] maintain that it is the rules themselves that maximise utility and that they ought to be followed even when a breach of them might be conducive to immediate utility. This manoeuvre enables the utilitarian to honour the significance of our intuitive moral judgements in his calculus, and rebut, to some extent, the charge that simple maximisation produces decisions repugnant to our moral sensibilities. Perhaps then, Ford and Nestlé should have considered the long-run benefits that accrue to business from the observance of certain constraints that are grounded in justice. Also, the interpretation of utilitarianism in rule-following terms avoids the charge often levelled against act-utilitarianism, i.e. it imposes impossible burdens on agents in the calculation of all possible consequences. Rule-following, on the assumption that the rules themselves have an established utilitarian value, is simply a way of economising on knowledge. If Nestlé had followed certain rules it might also have saved itself a lot of money. Though it is not absolutely clear that what the company did was 'wrong' by any of the established criteria of conduct.

However, the adoption of rule-utilitarianism for the solution to ethical problems in business is not without its disadvantages. Rules may be vague and indeterminate in particular cases and, more important, they may conflict. If in cases of conflict an appeal to beneficial consequences is used to settle conflicts then rule-utilitarianism simply collapses into act-utilitarianism. In the Nestlé case the rule that people are the best judges of their own interest clashed with the demand that products be made as safe as possible: it is not surprising, then, that the company thought that what it was doing was generally beneficial. More often than not ethical problems in business are ones that involve straightforward conflicts between profit-maximisation and ethical principles *per se*, as the Ford case illustrates in a spectacular way, and their resolution necessitates that the one give way to the other irrespective of various possible calculations in terms of well-being.

Deontological theories therefore claim that there should be constraints on human action that defeat all claims derived from utility. In fact, it is maintained that the moral autonomy of the individual is attenuated to the extent that his judgements are tainted by the thought of any consideration of satisfactions or beneficial consequences. In the history of moral philosophy there has been a variety of foundations for the apparent austerity of deontological ethics but for our purposes a brief indication of this style of thinking is all that is required.

In principle, deontological ethics rests on the claim that the right is prior to the good; that certain rules and practices, normally those that honour the integrity of the individual and encapsulate universal notions of justice, truth-telling and promise-keeping and so on, take precedence over well-being. It is these considerations that are brought to bear most heavily on businessmen engaged in the pursuit of profit.

At the heart of deontological ethics is an argument about the sanctity of the person: that no amount of goodness generated by an action can justify any violation of individual rights. This moral axiom (the Categorical Imperative) is expressed in a famous sentence by Immanuel Kant: 'Act so that you treat humanity, whether in your own person or in that of another, always as an end and never as a means only.'[21] This should not be misunderstood. It does not prohibit individuals using each other as a means to certain ends; almost all human interactions involve just this: none more so than the business relationship which is a complex network of people using other people's skills and endowments for their own ends. What the injunction does forbid, however, is their being merely used as a means to gratification: as the breach of a promise would, or the failure to disclose vital information prior to a purchase or an agreement. To place someone in slavery, even when it is to his own advantage (and some utilitarians have envisaged the justifiability of this, albeit in rare circumstances) would obviously be to breach the Kantian principle and hence to deny that each individual is an autonomous person.

It might superficially seem that deontological ethics would be hostile to business; that an activity driven by the profit motive and concerned primarily with the gratification of desires would fall short of the standards of the right. But this is not necessarily so, for deontological ethics is concerned only with the constraints that should obtain in whatever activity human beings engage in. A properly conducted business arrangement indeed exemplifies much of the deontological argument, especially in its emphasis on the obligatory nature of contracts and its recognition of the fact that each party is the author of his own actions. Indeed, many of those conventional rules that govern business, although they are often given a rule-utilitarian justification in the claim that business could not work without them, could just as easily be interpreted as constraints on action which have an intrinsic moral value.

Just Business

It is on the question of justice that many questions in the ethics of business turn; and the competing appraisals of both the business system and the behaviour of agents within it turn on widely divergent accounts of this crucial concept. It is important to remember that when people talk of the justice or injustice of business, profit and so on they have different exemplars of the concept in mind so that it rarely functions as a kind of Archimedean point against which competing claims can be evaluated. Nevertheless, it is true that the appeal to social justice which is often made by anti-business philosophers is an appeal to the most contested of moral concepts, and one which often bears only a remote resemblance to the original meaning of the term. It is also important to note that questions of distributive justice have little connection with business ethics: they are properly the concern of social philosophy.

The concept of justice that is most conducive to the business enterprise is one that is limited to the rules of fairness that ought to govern all human relationships: honouring promises, respecting the rights of justly acquired property (either through labour, exchange or gifts) and giving each person his due. It is not concerned with the 'outcome' of an economic process, i.e. the distribution of income and wealth that is generated by trade, but with the rules that govern it and the behaviour of individuals under those rules. Claims of injustice relate only to the intentional actions of persons under fair rules so that it would be illegitimate to condemn inegalitarian distributions of income and wealth as 'unjust'. Adam Smith argued that: 'Mere injustice is, upon most occasions but a negative virtue, and only hinders us from hurting our neighbour.'[22] Contemporary proponents of capitalism, such as Hayek, Friedman and Nozick, have added only sophistication to this fundamental proposition. Smith, and others, may have thought that these rules were sparse, and not descriptive of the 'good' society, but they were all that commerce required. They are often likened to the 'rules of grammar'.

It is a position that can have either a utilitarian or a deontological rationale. The utilitarian argues that to operate at maximum efficiency a market requires inequality of factor reward and that to sanction interference with this process by the invocation of abstract, external principles based on, for example (moral) desert or need, simply leads to the misallocation of resources. The rules of negative justice are simply those basic procedural devices that are required to make the market work efficiently: to guarantee security for property and contract and to provide a framework of predictability.

However, this rather simplistic utilitarianism is vulnerable to criticism when it is used to validate existing business practices. It is not entirely clear that the (sometimes) vast profits that are achieved in business, especially in the securities market, are required for the efficient working of the system. Market socialists have claimed, in a variety of complex schemes, that the efficiency properties of free exchange systems, and the freedom that markets grant to individual agents, can be reproduced without the excess profits and other imperfections that are said to characterise capitalist economies. Thus the existing business world and its practices may not be compatible with justice even when the latter is interpreted as a principle subordinate to efficiency.

However, it is not solely utilitarianism that sustains the theory of negative rules of justice: most writers in the free market tradition implicitly allude to the intrinsic value of fair rules. Hayek, for example, argues that socialism cannot be implemented without disrupting the rules of justice. The imposition of a rational plan can, he claims, come about only by the issuing of particular commands which will undermine the universality of just rules.[23] Furthermore, no matter how inegalitarian the outcomes of a market may be, they cannot be regarded as unjust because, in his view, injustice can only be the result of the intentional acts of responsible agents: the market, of course, is an impersonal, anonymous process. Again, Nozick, in a famous argument,[24] argues that the maintenance of a pattern of distribution, even if the morality of that could be agreed upon, would involve an unacceptable interference with people's choice, the undermining of the rule of law, and the use of individuals on behalf of collective ends. However, what makes these views vulnerable to moral condemnation is that they exclude reference to desert or worth in the understanding of economic justice; in fact inheritances or sheer luck are sources of entitlement as long as their rewards are achieved within the rules.

The critics of the capitalist system who use arguments derived from justice have a much more substantive concept in mind; they are less concerned about questions of efficiency anyway. Much of their argument derives from the deontological claim that the exchange system (and its associated framework of law and private property) exploits workers:[25] their autonomy to pursue their own ends is badly compromised by the wage-relationship, the existence of profit means that they do not receive the full value created by their labour, and the private owner makes little or no contribution to output (since he merely allows his capital to be used, his role is replaceable). Thus concepts such as desert and need become highly relevant to the distributional questions that are repeatedly asked of capitalist orders.

Although most questions of justice in relation to business are raised at the macro level, the validation of the whole system being one, problems can arise at the level of the individual enterprise. To what extent is a corporation under an obligation to practise 'affirmative action' in its hiring policies? Does not this lead to a conflict between efficiency and justice? Indeed, is not such a policy itself unjust? In most cases there is also the problem of a conflict between the duties that a management owes to its shareholders and the demands of social justice that are prescribed in much of business ethics. As I shall show, these problems are exacerbated when the rules of negative justice are expanded into a more substantive social doctrine. The injunctions of the protean doctrine of social justice are too vague, multifarious and incoherent to offer a precise guidance for individuals, even if it could be agreed that corporations and other business enterprises were under some obligation to act justly in the wider sense. None of this, of course, implies that the business imperative for management to safeguard the interests of shareholders, employees and consumers releases it from the obligation that everyone has to observe rules of fair play. There is a difference between an enterprise being under a moral duty and its being under a social duty.

When looking at business problems we tend to find a plurality of moral principles at work, with none providing determinate solutions. In this sense, business seems to reflect the moral dilemmas of everyday life. Although it would be hard to deny the (almost) compelling dictates of utility in normative economics, the principle itself does not have a monopoly in the ethics of commerce. It is often the case that consequentialist considerations ought to be constrained by moral rules. It is not good enough to say, as a rule-utilitarian might, that ultimately being ethical is good business: in the particular case it often may not. Thus to make certain principles absolutely binding would make the conduct of business virtually impossible. The moral injunction always to tell the whole truth would make advertising pointless yet there is a difference between deliberate deception and the making of exaggerated claims. But the difference is never clear. Certain tobacco companies (especially the Morris and Reynolds corporations) deliberately gave the impression in the 1950s and 1960s that cigarette smoking was not harmful to health: even though medical evidence to the contrary was mounting. Yet in other areas, evidence of moral culpability on the part of producers is much harder to demonstrate. The issue is further complicated by the fact that part of the liberal credo consists of a belief in the autonomy and rationality of the consumers, and that these features of human action themselves produce a check on the potential excess of business.

It is because of the difficulty of the direct application of moral principles to commercial life that an approach to business ethics has to take account of the circumstances of business enterprise. Commerce cannot require saint-like behaviour because we are not all saints (and if we were, to whom would we be saintly and what are the duties that saintliness implies?). The whole tradition of market economics, which maintains that good, utilitarian consequences can occur through spontaneous processes irrespective of the moral motives of the agents, is still an important starting point for business ethics. It is a kind of utility qualified by deontological rules: indeed Smith's *The Theory of Moral Sentiments*[26] is not a celebration of utilitarian ethics but a description of those rules of conduct that we apply to everyday conduct because they are felt to be 'right'. The structure of business ethics must not be about the foundations of 'rightness' but about the role of rules as restraints on egoistic actions in basically anonymous market orders. I have called this 'arm's length morality'.

Arm's Length and Minimalist Ethics

It is somewhat far-fetched to imagine that the actions of business agents should be directly guided by the kind of principles outlined above. These principles are best understood as criteria by which the actions of individuals are evaluated retrospectively by external observers. They are, if anything, ways of appraising the whole of business, and their application to particular cases may be hard to discern. Indeed, the disputes in business ethics themselves are not normally about whether, for example, utility is the only sustainable ethic but whether a particular action would enhance the well-being of the business enterprise. Again, the relevance of justice to commerce is not, surely, because some new distributive criteria may be discovered there but to understand if some particular action was fair or unfair by conventionally accepted standards of right conduct. The difficulty is that these standards are themselves infinitely contestable. Thus in the securities market the sometimes vast earnings that occur are condemnable as unjust, irrespective of the fact that these may have been achieved fairly, because they do not appear to be the outcomes of productive effort.

In many areas of business life, the standards and values of the market, which are broadly utilitarian, conflict with public morality. The latter has strong deontological elements: some actions are just not 'right' whatever the 'goodness' of the consequences that they bring about. This problem is compounded by the fact that public standards of morality are not only disputable in their application to particular cases but also they are relative to particular communities. For example 'bribery' in business is condemnable in Western capitalist economies but may be an integral part of social and business life in some communities. Can the deontologically based prohibition of it be applied incontrovertibly to international trade? The Lockheed bribery scandal of the mid-1970s is the *locus classicus* here.[27] The executives of the corporation bribed Japanese officials to secure a contract that (allegedly) 'saved' the investment of the stockholders and the jobs of the employees (utility). However, some people would say that the bribery was simply wrong, despite the utility gains it produced. The problem is that in Japanese society such action is not thought to be morally wrong (or even 'bribery'). What are companies to do in such circumstances? Abstract moral philosophy is not much help, though an ethics more closely related to the practice of business may be.

The reason for the failure of abstract ethics to give definitive answers is that the morality of business is comprised of a plurality of potentially conflicting principles, an unstable amalgam of possible explosive practices and maxims. It does not seem the type of activity appropriate for evaluation by rationalistic ethics. It is at best the ethics of self-interest, sanitised by the utilitarian claim that decentralised economic action does on the whole lead to better results for the anonymous public, and tempered by the restraints that deontological principles (imprecise though they are) impose on egoism. The notions of trust and honesty are relevant here: they are valued apart from their immediate utility. To the extent that business embodies them it is inescapably a moral enterprise.

In an important sense, business morality does differ from the morality of the family or that of small, closely knit communities. In these phenomena, ordinary egoistic action is restrained by principles of solidarity which are clearly understood and which can secure unanimous agreement: they are reinforced by the close proximity of the human agents. Despite the best efforts of some sophisticated neo-classical economists[28] to explain marriage as a contractual relationship in which gains from trade are made, and children are treated as a special type of consumer goods, our moral vocabulary is rich enough to differentiate between families and firms, and to indicate the diverging ethics that apply to each.

The obligations of family members are not 'self-assumed' (they are for the most part involuntary) while in business they clearly are: they are the voluntary obligations created primarily by contractual arrangements between strangers to advance their interests. There is no escaping this and a business ethics that underestimates it will (if 'legislated', as it frequently tends to become) systematically undermine the commercial enterprise. Of course, the formal agreements between individuals in basically anonymous markets have to be underwritten by moral rules and conventions which are not 'assumed' by agents, otherwise business would be uncertain. But these are of a minimal kind and in many ways are self-enforcing, or at least maintained by informal pressures. What this approach does imply is that extreme caution, if not outright scepticism, should be exercised in the face of demands that business agents should be encouraged or compelled to conform to values that emanate from outside the business relationship and the wider society; normally these extra-business values come from highly contestable social and political philosophies. Business is a moral enterprise that depends upon trust and honesty for its validity rather than the pursuit of all-embracing social goals, about which there can be little agreement: indeed it would be hubristic for business agents to suppose that they know what these are.

Business relationships in Western societies are conducted at 'arm's length', the participants do not in the main know each other and therefore can have no other duty but to respect their interests and the rules under which they exchange. Using this elementary model I shall cast doubt upon the possibility of 'contracts' between business and society since this presupposes that society can be represented as a determinate agent with a well-ordered and consistent hierarchy of values suitable for the exchange relationship: in fact, society represents a multiplicity of conflicting values to be realised and demands which press for satisfaction. I shall show that a properly structured set of legal and moral rules, situated in the business enterprise itself, may very well be the only means for 'solving' problems raised by a more activist business ethics.

It should also be noted that the more successful a business becomes in its fundamental aim, to provide cheap and reliable products through competition for the consumer (surely a moral enterprise in itself), the less 'fat' there will be for other activities, for example, charitable donations to worthy causes. Ironically, only monopolies, because of their 'immoral' and socially inefficient 'rents', will be able to comply with the more ambitious demands made by some business ethicists.

This suggested restriction of business ethics to the conduct of agents under rules appropriate to the commercial order, and expressed doubt about the wide social obligations of business, nevertheless leaves a host of very serious ethical problems. In Britain and the US the complaints and scandals that occur in commerce are precisely about breaches of what I have called minimalist rules. It is also the case that these rules do not apply solely to large-scale conglomerations. For although the moral indiscretions there are, for obvious reasons, likely to attract publicity, unethical conduct can occur in any relationship between strangers that is powered by self-interest. As the prominent American business ethicists Robert Soloman and Karen Hansen once pointed out: 'There is no reason to suppose that Mom and Pop's grocery store is any more moral than IBM'.[29]

A dominating principle inherent in this approach is the concept of *harm*. The most compelling of the negative obligations applicable to business is the injunction to refrain from damaging the interests of the trading partner: the crucial moral feature of the commercial order is voluntariness and it can be safely assumed that individuals do not voluntarily submit to actions that harm their interests. This is not to say that harm is the only consideration in the evaluation of business. An action may be adjudged right or wrong even if no one is harmed by it (for example, trade with South Africans could still be thought condemnable even though everyone gains from it); again, all people may gain from an action which was originally fradulent. But business could not go on without this minimum condition of non-harm being met. The strict prohibition of harm is the most important of the side-constraints on self-interested action and it is this that must constitute the primary element in a viable business ethics.

The difficulties with the notion of harm are exemplified in the debate about 'victimless crimes'; for many critics of the over-moralisation of business maintain that the current legal and moral persecution of insider trading in the stock market invokes precisely that. Indeed, in the recent Guinness scandal over share price rigging, it was not easy to identify the victims (but see pp 66–7) even though obvious criminal acts were committed. As we shall see, straightforward utilitarian and efficiency principles might well sanction insider trading yet people feel uneasy about it: largely, I suspect, because they are distressed by the particular distribution of rewards that comes from it. The minimalist conception of justice in the sense of fair rules (in which the 'no harm' principle occupies pride of place) clashes with certain deeply held and probably communally-based values of desert and merit. Even within the minimalist view, there may be disputes about what is or is not a fair contest, irrespective of the question of harm. The difficulty of identifying victims of alleged immoral practice has led to some business ethicists to claim that, irrespective of the absence of injured individuals, the business community has been harmed.

There are other equally important problems relating to the harm principle. Just as there are problems of identifying the victims of actions commonly held to be wrong there are disputes about the perpetrators of the wrong. Since business largely takes place through corporations which have a technical legal personality, and since commerce has strong features of a collaborative enterprise, it is often difficult to locate who is exactly responsible for a wrong.

The minimalist wants normally to locate responsibility for action in individual biological persons: they are the only agents, it is claimed, who can act with intent, an essential condition for legal and moral responsibility. Yet there has been a tendency, in the US especially, to make corporations legally liable for wrongs, as if a corporate agency were capable of criminal actions. The process began with the famous (but ultimately unsuccessful) prosecution of the Ford Motor Corporation for reckless homicide because of its failure to correct known faults in the Pinto car. Recently the Boeing Corporation was convicted of corporate crime. The nearest example in Britain was the prosecution of the P & O company for corporate manslaughter over the Zeebrugge ferry disaster. What was theoretically significant about this last case was the fact that the prosecution was allowed to go ahead: not the final result, which was an acquittal by the judge.

The moral problem raised by these cases is not so much the possibility that the prosecution of corporate bodies for criminal acts may be used to shield individuals from legal liability (in cases of corporate crime in Britain culpable individuals are prosecuted as well) but the meaningfulness of the claim that corporations can be treated as if they were moral persons. Arm's length business morality requires that praise and blame be attributed to identifiable, biological persons who are the only agents who can be said to be causally responsible for actions. A corporation is formally identified through its owners, the shareholders. Although they are in normal circumstances remote from the alleged wrong, it is they who have to pay the costs flowing from the wrong if the corporation is treated as a person.

I shall point out later the disturbing implications for business ethics that this growing legal phenomenon has. At this stage it is sufficient to say that it represents a dramatic departure from the individualism associated with arm's length morality: it substitutes collective for individual responsibility and hence blurs lines of moral accountability. It may even be said to replace justice with vengeance. From a strictly utilitarian position, corporations may be deterred from economically worthwhile activity if they knew that they were to be criminally liable for every action of their individual employees. Hence, many of the obvious economic advantages of the corporate form of organisation would be foregone.

Arm's length morality is concerned with agents exchanging their properties for their well-being, and exploiting whatever assets they might have in a rule-governed context in which rights are clearly specified. Ethical problems normally arise in those grey areas where property rights are in dispute and where the effects on third parties are neither clear nor quantifiable. This becomes especially important in the corporate form of organisation where the right to exclusive use of assets, especially knowledge, is indeterminate. Much of the dispute over insider trading arises from the doubt as to whether a company employee has the 'right' to use information for his own share purchases: it is always knowledge which he has not disclosed to the company's owners (the stockholders). Again, although it might justifiably be claimed that no one is harmed by insider trading, it is sometimes argued that the insider has an 'unfair' advantage over outsiders. The ethics that supports this contention obviously has a more expansive conception of justice in mind than that of arm's length morality: it is a substantive equality of opportunity that is being demanded rather than the equal application of common rules. But is this a feasible, even though it is widely held, moral principle?

Of course, arm's length morality may well sanction prohibitions of such trading through contracts between stockholders and employees that require immediate disclosure of all relevant information. On the other hand, the owners might not make such contracts, reasoning quite plausibly that they they will in fact gain more if employees are permitted to exploit knowledge that they have acquired working for the company (such permissions may be seen as a kind of reward in addition to salaries and other emoluments). There is the further moral claim that much of human activity in the workplace involves genuine entrepreneurial discovery, the fruits of which the discoverer is fully entitled (if his claim can be validated, which is not always easy).[30] Thus even within an arm's length morality serious ethical problems about ownership are likely to occur.

However, as I will show later, the difficulties with legislated business ethics are even greater in this area. For it is not at all clear what the ethical rationale for certain securities laws is. Is it the desire to create a 'level playing field' in financial markets? To enforce fiduciary duties on employees that perhaps would not have been contractually created? To define property rights independently of the act of discovery? One suspects that much of the moral anger directed against insider trading is derived from a form of Kantianism in which certain types of conduct are said to be intrinsically wrong irrespective of considerations of utility or of the morality of individual choice.

The final feature of arm's length morality is the emphasis it places upon individuals as independent and autonomous consumers, traders and other transactors in voluntary market relationships. It makes the somewhat ambitious claim that the market and the conventional legal system 'filter out' many of the problems identified by the more critical business ethicists. Hence arm's length morality contains a moral bias towards *caveat emptor* in all of its manifestations and a distrust of paternalism. Since much of business ethics consists of injunctions to government to provide protective services to persons who, it is maintained, would be helpless against, amongst others, corporations and advertisers, it is often in conflict with the arm's length tradition. It is *ipso facto* dissatisfied with the effectiveness of market mechanisms as a corrective to perceived moral wrongs committed by business personnel. It wishes to provide other remedies than those contained within civil and criminal law and the exchange system itself. It is, of course, true that we must have regulations in the business world, especially in product safety, in financial markets and in the environment precisely because the slowness of common law and the market in correcting wrongs in these areas means that many people would be harmed unnecessarily.

I should like to make two important disclaimers concerning the range of arm's length morality. First, I do not argue that it covers the whole of ethical conduct in business. There are occasions when business agents must take account of wider social obligations in their dealings and when duties that are more appropriate to the family, or the closely knit community, ought to intrude on relationships between strangers. Second, there is no suggestion in what I say that business values ought to be generalised across all aspects of social life. The deliberate promotion of the 'enterprise culture' by political authorities is as destructive of social life as it is of business life; indeed, the values of the latter are a spontaneous outgrowth of commercial society itself and cannot be replicated by governments.

What I attempt in the following pages is a reconstruction of a particular business ethic and an exploration of its strengths and weaknesses. It is important to do so since it has come under attack, ironically, at a time when former communist regimes are freeing themselves from an economic system which was powered by a quite different ethic. Many writers today make the case for a much stronger deontology of business than I am prepared to concede. However, the exposure of the limitations of the benign self-interest model is not the same thing as suggesting a viable alternative.[31] It may be regrettable that business is conducted according to a superficially unprepossessing ethic but in the Western world it is the prevailing value system and worthy of a hearing before it is condemned out of hand.

2 The Corporation

It is perhaps the modern organisation of economic activities, specifically the corporation, that has generated the demands for a special business ethics and for the 'moralisation' of commercial life. It is presumably because of the alleged privileged position that the corporation (especially its large-scale multinational mutation) occupies in society that questions about the propriety of its actions have been raised; and the power that it apparently wields has led to the attribution of special social responsibilities to it. Thus business ethics has come to be concerned not merely with individual conduct under general moral rules but increasingly with the special duties, normally of a non-contractual kind, that are said to belong to the business enterprise. Indeed, both in law and ethics, the corporation is being treated not merely as an aggregate of individual agents but as (almost) a biological 'entity', a moral agent that can be the subject of praise and blame.

The phenomenon of the corporation is therefore something of a problem for traditional liberal individualist ethics and economics. From John Locke to the present day liberal political philosophers have normally reserved typical ethical notions such as justice, responsibility, intentionality and so on, for individual actions only. The claim that aggregates (including corporations) can act was not only thought to be methodologically mistaken but productive of grievous moral error. The argument that large-scale collectivities such as nations and societies could 'act' and have a 'mind' in more than a meta-phorical sense, was not only thought to be a kind of metaphysical licence for an aggressive illiberal collectivism but also an opportunity for culpable individuals to evade moral responsibility for their actions. While the question of individual versus collective accountability received a dramatic airing in the context of international affairs, it has received a more modest but no less intellectually significant analysis in the world of business. The possibility of individuals hiding behind the 'corporate veil' to avoid responsibility for wrong-doing increases once it is accepted that a corporation can exercise real agency. Furthermore, if the corporation is a 'person' capable of performing 'wrongs' then the costs of this translation of individual action into collective action is inevitably borne by its owners, the shareholders who, in normal circumstances, are remote from the action in question.

The reason why there is now such an emphasis on corporate ethics is partly because of developments in economic organisation that have occurred in the last 200 years. When Adam Smith first celebrated the commercial order in

1776 he was writing about a competitive world inhabited by small enterprises, managed by their owners, and held together by simple legal rules, comprising property, tort and contract. The need for a separate commercial ethic was not apparent since the impact of commercial enterprise on society at large was not great. Indeed, Smith stressed that the simple negative rules of justice were all that would be required to service a commercial order, and the appeal to self-interest alone would be sufficient to supply men with essential goods and services.[1] That same motivation, and the competitive order itself, would also protect individuals from potential exploitation. Smith had some well-publicised doubts about the moral probity of the mercantile class itself[2] but these were not serious enough to justify government intervention on behalf of, say, consumers, investors, or society at large. Indeed, despite the temptations that existed for businessmen to collude, to fix prices and to act against the interests of the public, Smith still thought that the commercial ethic, with its features of autonomy, moral probity and prudence, was far superior to that of the soldier, aristocrat, or politician.

Furthermore, the ethics that the business system required were economical: they were the simple rules of justice and private property derived from the exercise of 'natural liberty' and those enjoining respect for persons as autonomous agents. Together they comprise arm's length morality. Although Smith believed that a virtuous society required the development of the more expansive moral notions of 'sympathy' and 'fellow feeling', he was in no doubt that a commercial order could function with these elementary rules. Justice, for example, required that individuals should refrain from damaging the interests of their neighbours, and this fundamentally negative view did not impose any special obligation upon commercial agents. Again, although Smith, in his moral writings, frequently referred to the 'impartial spectator' (or conscience) as the ultimate source of moral approbation and disapprobation, actions of which the spectator would disapprove need not necessarily be prevented by law. Only the rules of justice could be enforced by positive law. This leaves open the possibility that an action could be immoral but not strictly unjust. Contemporary business relationships are replete with examples of actions of this type.

However, legal and moral rules that may have been appropriate for the nascent capitalist order of the late eighteenth century are not conventionally thought to be adequate now. The rise of the large-scale corporation and the separation of ownership from control (a phenomenon that Adam Smith mistakenly thought would be inefficient,[3] irrespective of any moral problems that it might raise) has been viewed with suspicion even by apologists for capitalism and the market system. It is this that has led to the demands that business be socially responsible and fulfil moral obligations that are not normally expected of private citizens and small-scale proprietors. The latter's actions have no impact on the larger society and the duties of obedience to law and conventional morality which bind them are easily understood. Furthermore, these duties are attributable solely to discrete individuals.

However, Berle and Means, writing 150 years after Smith, claimed that:

> The concentration of economic power separate from ownership has, in fact,

created economic empires, and has delivered these empires into the hands of a new form of absolutism, relegating owners to the position of those who simply supply the means whereby the new princes may exercise their power.[4]

Implicit in this, and other similar observations, is the argument that normative political economy had not kept pace with changes in the economic system. The automatic checking mechanisms of the market, consumer choice and individual autonomy on corporate excess were thought to be inadequate, in an age of corporate power, to secure an identity between private and public interests. John Kenneth Galbraith's[5] claim that corporations dominated the private enterprise economy and that they were relatively immune from competition further fuelled the argument about corporate responsibility. At a more popular level than even Galbraith, Ralph Nader in the 1960s and 1970s led a campaign against the irresponsible managements of corporations, compared to whom shareholders and consumers were apparently powerless.[6] It was a powerlessness which was the main causal factor in the poor safety standards and contempt for consumer interests in many activities, especially the automobile industry. Unlike Galbraith, who thought that the corporation could not be reformed or moralised from within but had to be socialised, Nader pressed for the 'democratisation' of the corporation through government-sponsored shareholder power (including 'outside' representation on Boards of Directors to represent the public interest). However, Galbraith and Nader were at one in believing that corporate society could not autonomously develop an appropriate business ethics.

A further cause of complaint about the behaviour of corporations concerned the position of employees. In a world far removed from the ideal, fluid labour market in which individuals are free and autonomous because of the possibility of alternative employment, it was claimed that corporate society bound employees at all levels to the organisation. The alleged absence of a frictionless labour market meant that managements could, in effect, deprive employees of their civil rights. The many examples of 'whistle blowers' suffering for their exposure of corporate wrongs were enough to convince critics of the need for severe extra-market control of business: a need that has been successively reinforced by spectacular business scandals, such as the Ford Pinto affair in America, the Nestlé problem in the Third World and the thalidomide case involving Distillers in Britain. Arm's length morality, when located in the corporate world, seemed to display an alarming paucity in relation to what had become conventional ethical standards.

Many of the empirical claims of writers such as Galbraith have been found to be untrue under serious investigation;[7] the power of the corporation to manipulate tastes and to secure for itself immunity from competition has been grossly exaggerated and the independence of managements largely illusory. Competitive forces still operate as effective constraints, especially the market for corporate control which is a constant threat to managements. Furthermore, the separation of ownership from control does not incapacitate shareholders: the free exchangeability of stock in the securities market is a more realistic form of influence than direct management. Stockholders can also exert moral pressure too: witness the recent examples of disinvestment in South Africa. It is not obviously true that managements have a free hand or that they are immune from the ethical constraints that affect all interested individuals.

Nevertheless, these observations do not dispose of the moral questions raised by the existence of corporations or demonstrate automatically the applicability of an arm's length morality to business affairs. Ethical questions can be raised about business no matter how efficiently it is operating, and the obvious prevalence of self-interest on the part of shareholders is seen by almost all critics to be a strong inhibition to moral conduct. Most of all, the question of the extent of the social and moral responsibility of business in the context of modern conditions remains unanswered. For it is the nature of corporations that has provoked this question and has led to the claim that simple, Smithian morality is no longer enough. The corporation has, it seems, to be legitimised by something other than its economic success.

The Corporation and Its Genesis

The structure of the corporation is very much the same in all capitalistic legal systems. Whether it is a public or a private company it is normally characterised by a special form of the pooling of resources by individuals who, motivated by the desire for gain, want to use their assets in the most efficient way. It is characterised by limited liability, entity status, legal personality and perpetual life. It thus has all the features of an artificial person that in a sense exists apart from its (possibly) transient members. This image of personhood is embodied in the Board of Directors (who may or may not be shareholders) which takes decisions on behalf of its owners, the shareholders. It is normally the Board of Directors who are collectively and individually sued for any wrong-doing, even though the owners bear the costs of such actions. The important question here is the extent of the legal liability of the corporation. Does it include criminal liability? Or does the artifice of personhood preclude liability for actions thought to be possible only of biological agents?

The corporation, the legalised expression of the firm, is clearly a means to an end, the necessary organisational structure for the exploitation of resources. Superficially, its moral rationale is entirely utilitarian. I shall question whether its sole rationale is utilitarian later but at this stage it is important to indicate the significance of the corporate form for general economics. For in the nirvana of perfect competition there would be no place for such an obviously 'collectivist' institution as the firm or the corporation. Individuals would be fully informed, rational contractors who would costlessly trade with each other, without any intermediary institutions, to advance their interests.[8] No possibility of profit would exist since competition would instantaneously produce factor earnings exactly equal to their marginal productivity and equality in the possession of perfect information would prevent the exploitation of one agent by another. There would be no externalities and hence no problem of the attribution of responsibility to agents for causing, for example, pollution. Social and economic interaction under such ideal conditions would be the perfect example of arm's length morality. Although there might be moral problems about the initial distribution of assets from which such sanitised exchanges take place, these would be normative and political issues rather than value problems associated with exchange itself.

In reality markets are never like this; the economic world is characterised by uncertainty, lack of information and incessant change so that any movement towards market equilibrium (which does involve a plausible combination of efficiency and minimal justice) must involve human action, the exploitation of profitable opportunities and experimentation in various forms of economic organisation.[9] It thus generates the opportunity for a moral evaluation of human conduct in economic affairs. In particular the market process produces problems associated with the corporation and property.

The corporation or firm arises primarily because of the transaction costs that would confront individuals were they simply to exchange as atomised agents. It is easy to show that utilitarian reasons dictate that a system of specific contracts (there would have to be millions of these in an advanced economy) between isolated agents would be less efficient than a single contract binding the members of an organised group. In making such contracts individuals necessarily give up some of their liberties. Again, for utilitarian reasons, individuals would be less likely to undertake risky enterprises if they were liable for losses beyond the value of their resources invested in the organisation: hence the growth of limited liability. However, potential creditors could, in a free society, contract into different arrangements. These, and the other features of capitalistic economic organisation which are necessary for effective co-ordination in a world of uncertainty, generate 'profit' (income over and above marginal productivity) and possibly a form of 'power' for the more successful enterprises; even monopoly power for a few.

Historically, the most successful economies have been those that have developed forms of corporate organisation: but this utilitarian validation of capitalist enterprise has not been sufficient to establish its moral legitimacy. We have seen earlier that Western economic activity is validated by a plurality of moral principles in which deontological considerations involving justice, equality and the rights of persons compete with the utilitarian imperative. It is plausible to suppose that the competitive process involves a breach of these. The firm is a form of planning whose power over individual employees and society at large is only mitigated by the existence of other firms. Furthermore, the competitive process cannot completely eliminate the possibly immoral outcomes of some business activities, for example, the existence of corporate power, damage to the environment and avoidable effects on third parties, and the manufacture of unsafe products in the pursuit of profit. Indeed, in these areas, especially pollution, the more enterprises that there are, the worse (in a moral sense) the outcome of competition is sometimes likely to be. It is, therefore, in the absence of perfect competition that typical problems of business ethics arise.

The debate about the ethical responsibilities of the corporation has been informed by rival accounts of its origins; they are competing explanations which have differing moral and political implications. They are known as the 'legal creation' and the 'legal recognition' models. In the former, the corporation exists by permission of the state and its privileges are conferred on it by statute law.[10] The argument is that it could not exist without political authority.

It is not surprising that in this model the corporation is urged to give something back to society in return for its legally bestowed advantages. The duties that the corporation owes society at large are said to extend beyond those imposed by normal law and conventional morality (which apply to private individuals only). It is equally unsurprising that the proponents of this view should want to treat the corporation not merely as a legal entity subject to civil law but as a 'person' in the fullest sense and hence subject to moral praise and blame and, more importantly, capable of committing criminal acts. Though this last feature could be attributed to the corporation whatever its origin.

The overall rationale for this represents a curious combination of utility and deontology. Society approves of the corporation because it is an efficient economic form, the rewards that accrue to its members (employees and shareholders) are necessary to motivate them, and such privileges as limited liability are necessary for the growth of this efficient institution. However, all of this is legitimised by a kind of hypothetical 'contract' between business and society, the terms of which constrain not only the utility-maximising activities of its personnel on behalf of the interests of the larger society but which also embody principles of right conduct that bind individuals irrespective of any kind of utility. These principles, whatever they are, may be different from those that govern voluntary agreements.

The rival theory of the corporation, the legal recognition conception, traces its development to the spontaneous actions of individuals within the common law of property, contract and tort.[11] It is claimed that the familiar features of the corporation could be explained by an 'Invisible Hand' process in almost exactly the same way as the emergence of the 'money good' from the actions of decentralised agents has been explained. The pooling of resources, the creation of entity status and the collective liability for torts (though not crimes since these require a *mens rea* or 'guilty mind') are thus regarded as the consequences of individuals exercising their common law rights.

Perhaps the only interesting and controversial characteristic is that of limited liability. Although transactors would prefer liability to be limited to their investment in the organisation and their private assets protected, whether this occurs or not will depend on their mutual agreement. In fact, it is often claimed by proponents of this view that the conferment of the limited liability of corporations in statute law, in effect, licensed government supervision of business enterprise as a price for this privilege. The legal recognition model holds that political authority should be limited to confirming formally what has already taken place spontaneously. For example, some potential lenders to a business enterprise might not choose to transact under circumstances of limited liability (in some cases this does, of course, happen).

The upshot of this is that the special features of the corporation disappear and it is simply one of a number of enterprises that develop spontaneously out of a system of individualistic law and rights. Since the contractual arrangements are made between individuals, all rights and duties are owed to the very same individuals and none to society at large. The existence of the corporation, however, is also explained in deontological terms: people have rights to exchange, to co-operate and to use their resources as they wish within the confines of general law and morality, quite apart from the fact that the development of large-scale corporations has obvious efficiency advantages.

It is important to stress that the assumption of social responsibilities by corporations would not be excluded by the legal recognition model: whether there are any would depend ultimately on the owners of the assets of the corporation. Indeed, protagonists of the legal recognition model would claim that only these acts of social responsibility were genuinely moral actions since they could, presumably, involve the owners in a loss. What would be forbidden would be the compulsory performance of social duties by corporate executives without the agreement of the owners. Nevertheless, there is room for considerable dispute about the exact nature of corporate responsibility within the confines of the legal recognition model.

The history of the corporation is not strictly relevant to all this. Even though in English and American law the development of the corporation looks as if it depended on the action of the state, this does not prove that the state was logically necessary for it. Nevertheless, the debate about the social responsibility of corporations cannot be properly understood unless this distinction between legal creation and legal recognition is borne in mind. In Milton Friedman's famous essay on corporate responsibility he is implicitly describing a theory of the duties of corporate executives that arises out of his view of the corporation as a complex structure of voluntary contracts; a conception which embodies most of the points outlined above.

Friedman on the corporation

In his notorious essay 'The Social Responsibility of Business is to Increase Its Profits' (first published in 1970), Milton Friedman set the terms of the debate with his bold, and cogently argued, claim that business personnel had no moral responsibility to society at large beyond that of maximising the profits of the owners of the enterprise for whom they worked. However, a comprehensive reconstruction of Friedman's business philosophy depends upon not just this essay but his other work in normative political economy (especially *Capitalism and Freedom*, first published in 1962[12]). Friedman's theory of the social responsibility of business and his normative justification for capitalism are closely linked: taken together they constitute a single and distinctive approach to business and society.

His normative approach to political economy is well known. A decentralised private enterprise economy, in which individuals are motivated purely by self-interest, will generate a more efficient allocation of resources, one that is to the benefit of anonymous members of the public, better than any known alternative. Leaving aside the question as to whether this is true, the important normative claim that Friedman is making is that the public good is best advanced by a motivation (self-interest) which might be thought immoral by some popular standards of ethics. Of course, the theoretical and empirical evidence for the benign operation of the invisible hand is impressive and it forms a major part of capitalistic business ethics.

However, it leaves two crucial questions unanswered. First, is it true that everybody benefits from the market? Second, does its operation really conflict with conventional morality or is it at odds merely with the ethics of the saint or ascetic (or perhaps that extreme deontology that prohibits the slightest breach of justice even at the cost of immense utility gains)?

In answer to the first question I suspect that Friedman is a rough and ready kind of utilitarian. Although he does not write specifically about the problem of the inter-personal comparability of utilities (can the minor losses of some individuals be compensated by gains of others so that the greatest sum of utilities is generated?) it is clear that he views comparisons between rival economic systems in terms of aggregates rather than on their effects on known individuals. In aggregate, capitalism does better than socialism, even though its benefits might not be enjoyed by all individuals (and certainly not equally).

With regard to the second question, it is probably the case that Friedman's ethics are close to Adam Smith's: that is, he does not believe that profit-maximising behaviour is inconsistent with normal ethical values. It is only discordant with those of the ascetic (the political implementation of which would involve a violation of the not necessarily immoral freedoms of others). In a slightly mysterious phrase, Friedman says that the responsibility of business personnel 'is to conduct business in accordance with their desires, which generally will be to make as much money as possible while conforming to the basic rules of society, both those embodied in law and *those embodied in ethical custom*'[13] (emphasis added). But this last phrase is systematically ambiguous. For although it appears to impose some deontological constraints on profit-maximisation it is not at all clear what these are, or what they imply for particular cases. If profit-maximisation is to the overall benefit of society, then should not this economic imperative (utilitarianism) defeat all other claims? Or does it not? Again, is it permissible for a business agent to pursue a course of action which is not itself illegal but which may adversely affect others? The obvious example here is the production and marketing of dangerous products. These are questions to which I will return.

When he writes specifically of the corporation, Friedman appears to have the legal recognition view in mind: the corporation consists primarily of a complex set of contractual relationships between the owners, employees and customers. It is these that ultimately determine the responsibilities of corporate executives; there is therefore no contract of society that would enjoin any obligations that would fall outside such deliberately self-assumed duties. The model that Friedman explicitly has in mind is that of the principal–agent relationship. Corporate executives are employees and it would be a breach of their contractual duties if they were to spend corporate money on socially desirable projects of their choice. It would also be a usurpation of political authority since Friedman believes that Western democracies have adequate governmental machinery for the achievement of social aims. The latter must be ultimately determined by the voters.

It is also important to note that Friedman, along with other critics of the social responsibility of business, is disturbed by the fact that the business community has welcomed the pressure to adopt non-commercial criteria for the evaluation of their actions. This is especially true of corporate executives—who are not normally the owners of the assets which they are under an obligation to manage. They are quite likely to be tempted by the 'psychic' income which can be derived from extra-commercial activities. One doesn't have to be a fully fledged Mandevillian to be sceptical of the genuineness of socially responsible action by corporate executives when it does not (for them) involve a sacrifice of profitable opportunities on behalf of higher moral ends.

Friedman's doctrine has been much criticised, both from writers moderately favourable to business and those hostile to it. It has done much to sustain the 'myth of amoral business', though it is clearly a doctrine shrouded, albeit obscurely, in a certain ethics (utilitarianism). However, despite its admirable lucidity, in some areas at least it is not wholly clear what its prescriptions are. It is certainly an example of arm's length morality: agents are held together by the cash nexus and conventionally accepted legal and moral rules, and a distinction is drawn between the duties we owe to each other as strangers in the market and those we might have as members of families or as participants in some voluntary charitable enterprise. However, it is uncertain what this implies for some of the difficult moral decisions that face business personnel (and those who evaluate their actions). Conventional morality may often conflict with the utility-maximising imperative, within which the responsibility of business to increase its profits is contained, and this is largely because conventional morality encompasses non-utilitarian elements.

The lack of clear guidance for business in Friedman's approach derives from his failure to distinguish between two aspects of the social responsibility thesis. One is a positive injunction addressed to commerce to fulfil certain alleged desirable social goals, the other is the imperative that it should refrain from certain actions that are profit-maximising in a crude sense but which also involve risks and harm, either to individuals or to the community. An exposure of the economic and moral implausibility of the first claim does not entail a refutation of the second. Furthermore, a failure to make this distinction tarnishes the overall reputation of arm's length morality.

There is the further implication that Friedman regards the rules of conventional morality as mere constraints which profit-maximisers must be aware of and which limit their activities. Thus they are not expressive of a genuine business morality but simply costs which confront transactors. To treat them in this way is perhaps to drain them of their true moral significance and to encourage traders to meet only the minimum standards. I do not think that this necessarily follows, but the iconoclastic nature of Friedman's argument has lent a certain credence to this view.

The Social Responsibility Thesis Examined

The claim that business ought to restrain its profit-maximising activities by, for example, refusing to raise prices in a forlorn attempt to beat inflation, or to pursue rigorously non-discrimination policies in the workplace so as to secure a racial and sexual balance, to provide 'welfare' facilities for its employees at the cost of profits and jobs, to make charitable donations of shareholders' money to favoured causes and so on, are activities which are clearly political rather than economic. They may advance the prestige of corporate employees but they are morally dubious and, in most cases, economically inefficient. To the extent that such activity is moral it can at the most only enjoin supererogatory (desirable but not compelling) duties. If there are such moral duties, they can arise out of a general social philosophy (addressed to government), not from the practice of business itself. It is morally arbitrary to impose them on the business community but not on others.

Of course, if the owners of corporations wish their money to be invested in this way there can be no objection; except that in America charitable donation by business is often done for tax reasons rather than from a genuine moral motive. If such activities are pursued by executives of a corporation they do not involve genuine moral action, for they (the executives) do not have to bear the costs that they entail. Genuine ethical actions must involve choice; usually a choice between the obligatoriness of an ethical principle and the lure of profit.

Although there may be some truth in the claim, made by virtually all business ethicists, that good and virtuous business is profitable, this only applies to the practice of business overall. The real problems occur in those particular cases which often do present difficult choices between morality and profit for agents. These problems arise in the context of the second, or negative, aspect of business ethics: the injunction to avoid harm and to sacrifice profits for the sake of other people's rights. They do not arise in the cases of corporate executives pursuing worthy ends for which they do not bear the costs.

In any event, the latter activity is almost certainly doomed to failure because of the nature of a competitive economy. The first duty of agents (corporate executives) is to use the assets over which they have direct control efficiently for the benefit of the owners; and hence, indirectly, for the benefit of the consumers. This is a duty sanctioned by arm's length morality and by the ultimate validating principle of utility. However, since excessive use of a company's assets for social purposes is certain to reduce profit and the consequent fall in the value of its shares, a takeover is likely. Indeed, executives are in breach of their duty to shareholders if they behave in the way described because then the assets of the company are misused. No amount of talk about the disjuncture between ownership and control can distort the fact that others in the commercial enterprise will exercise their rights to sell their shares in a company that is being mismanaged. The more competitive an economy is then the less opportunity exists for the fulfilment of supererogatory duties. In fact, such duties can only be exercised by those owners who don't mind taking a loss. In sum, there is a conflict between the demand that an economy be more competitive (an injunction which is validated by utility) and the claim that business has social duties that extend beyond the rules of arm's length morality.

In fact, only in a monopoly is there that amount of 'slack' sufficient to make the performance of these extra duties at all viable. Even here, they would lie more heavily on the owners than on the corporate executives, who still remain under their conventional contractual duties. Even when the owners perform social duties, one suspects that it is hardly a moral act at all: it is much more likely to be a tactical manoeuvre to prevent government regulation (or nationalisation) of the monopoly in question, or the taxing away of its 'rents'.

In fact, many of the alleged moral duties of corporations defeat the purposes of a market economy (and furthermore render it highly vulnerable to regulation). An example is the 'voluntary' agreement of business enterprises to control wages and prices in battles against inflation. The misallocative effects of this are well known but the moral implications of the strategy are less often articulated. For it distracts attention away from the institution which is morally responsible for inflation in the first place, government. Government exhortation, to both employers and unions, to restrain their actions on behalf of the community, is in fact pointless and is invariably followed by something much more sinister, direct government involvement in prices and incomes.

Where corporate policy involves the sacrifice of profitability for social duties it more often than not entails a selective attitude towards the potential beneficiaries of its generosity. Henry Manne[14] quotes the instructive example of Coca-Cola's attempt to provide a kind of private enterprise welfare system for its employees who were working in rather poor conditions in Florida (they were immigrants who had made the calculation that however bad their conditions were while working for Coca-Cola they were at least better than the alternatives facing them in their home countries). The result of Coca-Cola's benevolence was, of course, an increase in their costs and therefore a reduction in employment opportunities. Yet all the moral attention was focused on the welfare scheme, and none of it on those unknown people who had been made unemployed by it.

One of the features of arm's length morality, indeed any coherent ethical system, is that its rules should be impartial between all affected agents. The more that supererogatory duties are imposed on business the less likely it is that this basic condition of morality can be met. Actions such as those of Coca-Cola may be 'good business' (or at least good for *its* business) but in that case good business may be bad ethics. In all of these matters it is surely the responsibility of government to act (at the behest of the voters) rather than private individuals engaged in a quite different enterprise.

Economic activity involves the constant reallocation of resources in order to meet more effectively consumer demands: that it is powered by self-interest (from shareholders, employers, employees and all other interested parties) is a more or less immutable fact of the human condition which it would be naive to ignore. Indeed, the attempt to alter such motivations has historically proved to be extremely costly. It is certainly true that (in Schumpeter's phrase) 'the gales of creative destruction' that accompany competition leave many 'innocent victims' in their wake, but it is difficult to maintain that this is a moral problem which it is the duty of business to solve. It my be a supererogatory duty which the *owners* of enterprises may wish to fulfil (just as the same agents may refrain from certain sorts of investment for moral reasons[15]) but the assumption of a welfare role by managements is to confuse politics and economics to the detriment of both.

The claim that corporations, either through their owners or managers, have wider social obligations than those prescribed by arm's length morality derives largely from the doctrine that they exist by 'permission' of society; as if there is a social contract between business and the community which validates commercial activity and sets the terms under which business is to operate.[16] Such a contract must, of course, be hypothetical since it is scarcely conceivable that the whole structure of business and social relationships could spring from some single act of agreement. Yet the idea itself is not entirely fanciful: we do consider ourselves in moral relationships to be bound by rules which we accept even though we never formally pledged our allegiance to them. In this context, to say that business activity is limited by conventional moral rules is perfectly reasonable. But it is much more controversial to suppose that this hypothetical contract permits corporations to exist only if they fulfil certain contentious social purposes. The corporation evolved out of the framework of conventional law and morality and possesses no rights that individuals do not possess and therefore no duties that do not also apply to other agents. Indeed, the fact that positive law confers limited liability is unfortunate, since it gives credence to the argument that this feature depends exclusively on the state, which in turn morally licenses political control of business.[17] This is, of course, a form of control that extends beyond the enforcement of those rules that apply to all individuals.

When corporations, through the permission of their owners, voluntarily assume special burdens, such as the imposition of racial or sexual quotas in the workforce, disinvesting in immoral activities and foregoing alternative profitable opportunities in plant relocation policies, there can be no objection on ethical grounds (or, indeed, efficiency grounds since these altruistic actions are the product of genuine choice). However, if this duty is imposed on managements it not only provokes a moral conflict between their duties to the shareholders and their social obligations but also creates a dissonance between the ideal of competition (which surely has its virtues) and that of social benevolence. The latter problem is seldom appreciated by business ethicists who seem unaware of the obvious fact that extra-market activities impose costs on corporations which render them vulnerable to takeover by less socially conscious individuals in the endless process of change that competitive capitalism generates.

It is perhaps a recognition of the above dilemma that faces managements which has led some business ethicists to recommend the (statutory) appointment of 'outsiders' (that is, personnel neither from the management nor from the legal owners) on to the boards of public companies.[18] Presumably, if the necessary conditions of competitive markets make it impossible for the managements of corporations to perform their social duties, and act for a public interest which is somehow different from that which emerges spontaneously from the actions of decentralised agents, then an artificial remedy is required. Although this is not yet a feature of public policy it has figured prominently in the texts of business ethics. Some go so far as to suggest that a majority of a Board of Directors should consist of 'outsiders'.

To anyone familiar with the mechanics of a market economy this suggestion is sinister: it derives a superficial plausibility only from the widely held, but erroneous, view that because a market system is driven by self-interest it is incapable of generating the public good. Since most socialist regimes are now struggling to introduce private property-based market systems embodying this same motivation, the initial plausibility of the claim looks less than convincing. Theoretical and empirical evidence need not be reproduced here to demonstrate the economic virtues of the system: it is sufficient to repeat the point that the most efficient use of assets is achieved through private owners who are responsible to the public through the marketplace. The substitution of public decisions for private decisions, as would happen if outsiders controlled Boards of Directors, would not guarantee that the interests of the public would be maximised. In these circumstances the enterprise system would be politicised, and its activities would be dictated by partial interests in society. No evidence is produced by the designers of the schemes to show that the restraint on the profit motive that they entail would be socially beneficial. Still less is there likely to be general agreement on what this extra-market public interest is.

Since the proponents of the schemes are not recommending the wholesale replacement of capitalism by a *dirigiste* economic system, but rather grafting on to it alleged desirable institutional arrangements that are not spontaneously generated, it is incumbent on them to consider the question as to whether such a revised capitalist system could possibly function. There is indeed a plurality of conflicting principles at work in the evaluation of conduct in a free society: in the business world this is normally exemplified in the irresolvable disharmony between the competing claims of efficiency and the restraints imposed by the varieties of deontological principles that people hold. It is by no means obvious that restraints on profit maximisation are better achieved by politically inspired organisational changes than by the rules of the common law and conventional morality.

There is, however, more than a grain of truth in some other moral criticisms of the corporation; for often the desire for profit does produce actions which offend against deeply held moral principles. However, I suggest that these are much more to do with sins of commission (for example, the deliberate production and marketing of unsafe products) than with omission (for example, the failure to invest in areas of high unemployment). The latter are supererogatory duties, if they are duties at all, and the opportunities for their fulfilment are necessarily limited in a competitive economy. There is, then, a distinction between the 'social audit' and the 'moral audit': a difference between the failure to perform infeasible social duties (about which there is little possibility of agreement in an open society) and the refusal to conform to those basic moral constraints that bind all rational agents. The question is whether an arm's length morality is sufficient to ground a sustainable but limited business ethics in the face of the conflicting demands of profit and justice.

The Corporation and Moral Wrong

As already noted, the weakness in Friedman's rejection of the social responsibility of business thesis is that, although he admits that profit-maximisation ought to be constrained by conventional morality, he does not indicate what this is, or point to any principle which might adjudicate between the imperative of efficiency and the claims of justice when these two antagonistic principles collide. Since some of the interesting business scandals do not involve explicit law-breaking, either criminal or civil, they necessarily involve the question of how far particular corporations should observe non-enforceable standards when they cannot guarantee that others will be so virtuous.

The typical problems occur in the environment and in the question of product safety. In the former, the possibility of market corrective processes filtering out immoral practice is unlikely to occur since the harm involved is (normally) to unidentifiable agents. Indeed, in the question of pollution it is not always possible to identify the wrongdoer since pollution is not necessarily bad, but is an unavoidable consequence of (valued) high productivity; it is the *extra* firm(s) that generates a social and economic conundrum.

I think that if we look at the standard examples of immoral conduct by business we shall find that the activity in question is condemnable by ordinary commonsense morality and that the criticism does not derive from a full-blown moral philosophy in which each ethical decision is a logical deduction from a self-consistent set of axioms, but from non-philosophical reflection on the nature of just conduct. The ethics of business in this theory is simply the ethics of the prudent man: it echoes perhaps the moral sound of Adam Smith's 'voice within' (or conscience) that tells us that some action is morally wrong.[19]

It is necessarily an ethics that is conditioned by known cultural attitudes and mores. The latter point is crucially important because it cautions a certain modesty in those who would universalise Western moral values across divergent cultures. The obvious example here is 'bribery': a tricky concept that encompasses a range of actions, from culturally expected friendly gifts to outright corruption. It cannot be known in advance which actions on this wide spectrum are morally condemnable. It will depend on the compelling nature of communal values rather than the injunctions of a universal morality.

What I have called arm's length morality is no more than the business exemplification of this ethical modesty. It assumes that agents in business are engaged in an enterprise in which self-interest is unavoidably prominent but not exhaustive of all behaviour. The only special consideration, one that might be exclusive to the business enterprise, is that an arm's length morality assumes a certain (but difficult to specify) amount of autonomy and responsibility on the part of participants in the business game. Advertising is not supposed to deceive, yet at the same time no one would expect competing firms to tell the exact truth about their products: this is a subjective area where persuasion is surely legitimate. The concept of *caveat emptor* ('buyer beware') is addressed to responsible agents capable of making informed choices. Although this does not excuse producers who wilfully manufacture faulty products, it does encourage a sceptical attitude towards the petty and paternalist regulations of recent years which, in a desire to help the consumer, often makes goods needlessly expensive or unobtainable. Again, the idea of responsibility has a cultural dimension, for the prudent businessman will place less reliance on autonomous choice in dealing with consumers in countries of generally low educational standards and poor economic conditions.

From the above preliminary observations it is possible to analyse critically recent familiar examples of corporate misbehaviour.[20] We shall notice that the kinds of wrong-doing identified are not exclusive to business but can equally occur in other 'professional' activities, such as politics and the law. The only reason why business attracts such bad publicity is that it is founded upon a feature of human motivation, self-interest, which has had such a bad moral press throughout history.

When the Ford Motor Company manufactured the Pinto car, which was known to be faulty, in the late 1970s, it was clearly in breach of the moral standards set by arm's length morality. Although it may be true to say that there is 'no such thing as a safe product' it is true in a trivial sense only, and although it is also true that the search for perfect safety would price most products out of the reach of ordinary people, the circumstances in which the Pinto was manufactured indicate a clear lack of concern for potential customers. An attitude which was condemnable by any standards of morality. The executives simply did a cost-benefit analysis of the probable costs of civil actions in the event of an accident compared with the costs of correcting the fault. Ford did not in fact make a utilitarian judgement, since a fully fledged consequentialist evaluation of conduct requires that the interests of *all* parties be taken into account (including, in this case, potential victims), difficult and contentious though that may be. A serious accident eventually occurred in which a number of people were killed.

Only a morally insensitive libertarian ideologue would maintain that the problem would be solvable by appropriate warning signs and disclaimers on the part of the producers of such blatantly unsafe products. It is true that there is no demand for completely unsafe products (the market itself drives out obvious immorality) but the problems invariably arise at the margin. They also arise, as with the Pinto, when third parties are adversely affected by the actions of individuals who might themselves be prepared to take risks with unsafe products. In the Ford case, the competitive instinct drove the corporation clearly to the wrong side of that indeterminate and vague line. It is not that business ethics in such cases tells us what is right, but the commonsense morality which tells us what is wrong.

However, there are perhaps two ethical problems that emerge from this and similar cases of immoral conduct which have a special connection with business. The first concerns the identity of the wrong-doer. Are the individual agents who took the decision responsible or does a form of corporate liability lie on the company itself? I shall deal with the vexed question of individual versus collective responsibility in the final section of this chapter. The second problem is that the very anonymity of market society may weaken those restraints on self-interested action that we expect to apply to business. The fact that we do not know the people with whom we deal increases the temptation to treat them merely as a means to our own ends: an attitude which is often sanitised by a loose and insensitive application of the liberal principle of personal responsibility.

Limitations of Arm's Length Morality

The application of a pure arm's length morality to business might well sanction the concealment of all but the minimum information about a product; it would exclude only deliberate deception and leave the individual to make his own judgement. Yet a producer would be likely to inform a relative or close friend much more about a particular product precisely because a different morality is appropriate in those contexts. Would a Ford executive have concealed from his grandmother the truth about the Pinto? It is never clear how far such moral attitudes should pervade the business relationship but commonsense ethics suggests that where danger is involved it would be a breach of the simplest deontological principles to treat anonymous customers differently from those who are part of a close network of personal relationships. Thus arm's length morality should always be checked and controlled by wider moral principles.

The moral questions turn on how much information has been revealed about particular products and how much of it an individual is entitled to when making a purchase. Some of this information is, of course, revealed in the price, and in many circumstances this is all that is required: the market will have sifted out any extra moral complexity. It is an assumption of market theory that, for a choice to be 'rational', it must be fully informed, but in conditions short of perfect competition this heady requirement cannot be met: in fact ongoing competitive arrangements are characterised by the constant search for new information. The moral framework of business is controversial because of the irresolvable clash between the potentially paternalist and costly regularity imperative and the individualist's plea for personal autonomy and responsibility for consumers.

The problem is no better exemplified than in the issue of cigarette smoking and advertising. Tobacco companies have been a favourite target of business ethicists ever since the invention of business ethics. An extreme deontological argument would imply that it is simply immoral to permit an apparently life-threatening activity to continue, despite the mutual satisfactions derived from the trade between the tobacco producer and consumer. But few moralists would forego the losses in utility (and freedom and responsibility) that an outright ban would entail. Yet undoubtedly, an arm's length business moral-ity leaves many people uneasy; especially as the activities of tobacco com-panies are designed to attract young people (to whom the notions of responsi-bility and personal autonomy perhaps do not yet apply) into a dangerous addiction which swells corporate revenues. Hence, the moral issue is really about advertising and the information that it conveys.

In the 1950s and as late as the 1960s, the major US tobacco companies, Philip Morris and R J Reynolds, did not merely advertise their product, they marketed smoking as a health-enhancing activity![21] It was claimed that cigarette smoking did not cause the diseases that scientific research was revealing and that it had positive physical and psychological advantages. For example, Kent cigarettes (in comparison with other brands) were advertised as 'the greatest health protection in history' just at the time when their tar and nicotine content was being increased. Not surprisingly, successive advertising campaigns have met with hostile criticism. However, without defending the tobacco companies, it should be pointed out that much of the evidence of their deception is not completely convincing since it was adduced from the period prior to the full realisation of the dangerous effects of smoking. Ironically, some of the claims made were actually true: for example the much vaunted claim that 'more doctors smoke Camel than any other cigarette'.[22] In Britain, too, doctors at one time had higher smoking rates than other groups. But is it legitimate for advertisers to manipulate such double-edged truths? Still, it is worth pointing out that, in an unusual tribute to the notion of *caveat emptor* and personal responsibility for action, the US judiciary has consistently refused to uphold claims for damages against tobacco companies.

Obviously, the question of 'truth' in this type of advertising is infinitely contestable, and the claim of personal responsibility for action is often stret-ched in the face of known dangers. It is noticeable that governments are by no means unhypocritical. They have not actually banned smoking but they have made the advertising of it extraordinarily difficult. I suspect that this is not merely because they want the tax revenue from tobacco sales (govern-ments are not exactly uninventive when seeking new sources of income) but because of the difficulties that emerge when two equally plausible principles conflict: the imperative of personal responsibility for action and the desire to protect people from their own folly.

Also, it is possible that governments' attempts to restrain the activities of corporations on moral and legal grounds will ultimately prove to be less effective than informal measures. The recent decline in smoking has surely been as much to do with negative consumer pressure, and a social atmosphere hostile to the activity, than it has with overt government propaganda. And, anyway it does seem immoral for political authorities to put all the blame on corporations when the latter are simply responding to consumer demand. Actually, the moralism of informal group pressure is more worthy than political campaigns against corporations, since at least the former is directed against individual smokers. Furthermore, the 'externality' argument (that smokers do not merely harm themselves but affect innocent third parties) is more manageable when used in this way.

The moral force of personal responsibility was less persuasive in the Nestlé case in which mothers in Third World countries misused the 'infant formula' (powdered milk).[23] Deaths of babies occurred largely because of lack of information, and adverse economic conditions caused mothers to over-dilute the formula, often with contaminated water. It is slightly different from the cigarette case because it was obviously not suggested that the formula was harmful: it is only potentially so if it is used incorrectly. Nestlé was singled out for criticism because it continued to market the product when it was revealed by various health organisations to have harmful effects under certain circumstances. Nestlé was accused of blatantly ignoring the authoritative warnings of the World Health Organisation.

It is not difficult to mount a defence of Nestlé from a straightforward utilitarian perspective, this is indeed what the corporation did in the face of organised protests and boycotts. The company argued that the social benefits outweighed the costs; indeed it is plausible to suggest that they did. Furthermore, Nestlé could not be held responsible for the misuse of their product as there was no clear deception in its marketing and advertising. Were they not treating the consumers as autonomous agents capable of making rational choices? However, certainly a broadened utilitarianism would have taken account of the possible harmful effects on a minority in its use of the formula. It would be a morally crass form of cost-benefit analysis that permitted the gains (however massive) of the majority to over-ride completely the harms caused to a minority (however small). Furthermore, it would certainly not be inconsistent with utilitarianism to take account of the informational disparities between various sets of consumers.

It would therefore be possible to regard Nestlé's action as condemnable from that version of arm's length morality which is primarily utilitarian in emphasis. However, the major criticism of Nestlé was grounded in a much more controversial deontological framework. The corporation was actually accused of violating the rights of mothers in the Third World by continuing to market the product in the face of mounting unfavourable evidence. Apparently the competitive impulse and the desire for profit had been decisive over all other considerations. The consumers had been used only as a means to the end of corporate commercial success. This seems a much more contentious case, for there was nothing in Nestlé's actions that specifically violated the rights of individuals and, indeed, a genuine deontological ethics would not turn upon the material interests of individuals as perceived by outsiders but upon a recognition of their personal autonomy. It is rather odd to describe restraints, either voluntary ones exercised by the corporation or compulsory regulation by the state, as rights-enhancing since a market transaction which leaves the consumer to make up his own mind is an expression of individual choice and autonomy.

The morality of corporate action in many of its activities turns upon the type and extent of information which is relevant to consumer choice. In a perfectly competitive market, with its assumption of complete information, no consumer could ever be exploited. But the real world is characterised by varying degrees of informational scarcity and, since profit is achieved by the exploitation of imperfect knowledge, moral problems arise: problems which are exacerbated by the anonymity of the exchange process in complex industrial societies. But do they require a special business ethic for their resolution or does ordinary morality (and indeed, common law) suffice?

One suspects that in the classic examples of corporate misbehaviour the actions are condemnable by the morality of the prudent man. For example, the Johns-Manville Corporation[24] continued for many years to manufacture asbestos products which the company knew to be dangerous for their workers (the process caused a serious lung disease, asbestosis): the true extent of the health hazard was concealed from their employees. Still, as it turned out, the corporation was eventually all but ruined by successful civil actions.

Nevertheless, there does seem to be something different about the morality of business. In its classic mode, the arm's length commercial contract is an instantaneous agreement, the consequences of which may come to be regretted later. It therefore places tremendous burdens of choice and rationality upon individuals; responsibilities which are less present in the intimate, 'face-to-face' relationships of the family and the small community. In the latter there are normally 'internalised' moral rules of a more substantive, and indeed long-term, kind, which are more or less independent of immediate gratification. The moral task of the corporation is to develop moral rules which in some way mimic these practices without at the same time undermining those (not necessarily immoral) motivations on which the success of the enterprise depends. It is perhaps the failure of the corporation to develop such a morality which has exposed it, in the twentieth century, to excessive regulation: to the costs of consumers and workers as well as shareholders. It is a political attack that is in part encouraged by the dubious claim that the corporation was created by the state. Thus, a thoughtless and short-term stress on individual autonomy in the marketplace may result paradoxically in the progressive whittling away of these crucial features of individuality.

Corporate Crime

Given that corporations do sometimes act wrongly there is a further ethical question: who exactly is responsible for corporate misbehaviour? The corporation is a legal personality liable for torts and any other civil wrongs committed in the course of its operations. There is nothing controversial in the arrangement whereby individuals, through pooling their resources in order to pursue commercial gain, make themselves liable in civil law for the possible costs that might be incurred in business. The fact that the owners (as the principal) and the Board of Directors (the agent) ultimately bear the costs of civil action is neither inconducive to efficiency nor offensive to morality. The separation of ownership and control theoretically makes no difference, for the entrustment of corporate assets to managements necessarily involves risk. Indeed, the possibility of civil action is an incentive for shareholders to take a more active interest in the affairs of the companies that they formally own.

In theory, the rights and duties of the corporation derive from the rights and duties of individuals. In practice, however, the development of the modern corporation, and its alleged social and economic power and immunity from corrective competitive processes, has led to the demand for a greater control over its activities than that provided by civil law and the market. Hence, the growth in the past few years of criminal prosecutions of corporations (for which managements take the 'blame' but shareholders pay the costs). Undoubtedly, the theory that corporations are the creatures of positive law, with its strong implication that the corporation is something more than a legal artifice constructed solely out of the legal rights of concrete individuals, has been influential. If this is so, then it would be possible to make a *prima facie* case for subjecting the corporation to duties that do not arise from the actions of individuals. A corporation could be treated as more than a legal artifice. It is perhaps a 'real' person of whom one could predicate actions independently of the actions of its individual members (for example, its board members and employees). Superficially, it sounds bizarre to speak of a corporation as an artifice capable of performing actions normally thought to be only possible of biological persons but there is some impressive philosophical literature on the subject of corporate personality.[25] It has some relevance to the rather prosaic question of whether it is legitimate to prosecute corporations for manslaughter, theft or any other serious criminal offence.

In neither law nor morality has the question of corporate criminal responsibility been solved, though the issue has been given a much more thorough airing by lawyers and philosophers in America than in Britain. The first serious example of alleged corporate responsibility for crime was the prosecution of the Ford Motor Corporation for reckless homicide in 1980.[26] Of course, criminal responsibility had previously been attributed to corporations, both in Britain and the US, but this had been for less serious (and less obviously personal) offences: normally those which lie on the borderline between torts and crimes. Although Ford's original defence to the charge of reckless homicide, i.e. a corporation is not a person and cannot commit manslaughter, was rejected, it was eventually acquitted at the trial. Nevertheless, there have been some successful prosecutions of corporations for criminal offences, the most recent resulted in fines and restitution totalling $5 million being imposed on the Boeing Corporation for a two-count felony. The example of the unsuccessful prosecution (1990) of the P & O Company for corporate manslaughter over the deaths involved in the Zeebrugge tragedy is close to the American models. In English law it has been established that corporations can be charged with crimes which were once thought possible only of biological agents but as yet the conditions for success are extraordinarily difficult to satisfy.

Irrespective of how the law develops, the question of corporate liability for serious crime raises fundamental ethical (not to mention philosophical) issues. Can the notion of intention and *mens rea* (a guilty mind) seriously be attributed to non-human agencies? Who are the people to be considered as representative of the corporation in such actions? What kind of penalty is appropriate when the offence has been proved? Should shareholders, who normally have nothing to do with criminal action (individuals who own corporations do not normally set them up in order to commit crimes!), have to pay the heavy fines that result from convictions? Is it likely that an increase in, and extension of, corporate liability will make it easier for culpable individuals to hide behind the 'corporate veil'? Finally, and of growing importance, does the criminal prosecution of corporations reflect a desire for 'vengeance' in response to horrific accidents rather than a concern for justice?

The claim that corporations can act intentionally and have a guilty mind arises out of a proposed distinction between an 'aggregate' and a 'conglomerate'.[27] An aggregate is merely a set of individuals who may do things together which they could not do separately; but it does not constitute a permanent, ongoing entity capable of being identified independently of these discrete individuals. However, a conglomerate has the feature of permanance and it exists irrespective of the changing composition of its membership. It is identified not by the attitudes of particular individuals but in its collective biography, or record of its aims and purposes, successes and failures. American business ethicists tend to locate the separate identity of the corporation with the Corporate Internal Decision Structure or CIDS (which contains basically its fundamental *telos*, or state at which it aims). This identification enables us to say that the corporation can 'act' and hence exhibit intention and responsibility. Nevertheless all writers who take this position do say that it still requires some individual endeavour to activate the CIDS.

Now it is true that many organisations (and not only firms) have a life that transcends the lives of individual members, and we do often speak metaphorically of collective minds. It is also true that individuals can do things in concert, both good and bad, which they cannot do as individuals. The whole nature of the corporation presupposes that part of its essence is that it has a life beyond the lives of its individual members. The identity of corporations cannot be established by knowledge of the identities of its individual, and possibly transitory, members.

However, none or all of these features together are sufficient to justify the claim that corporations can act intentionally in the way that humans can. Or that they can experience shame, regret, remorse and so on. In fact, business philosophers systematically misunderstand the nature of the business enterprise. It is a means to an end, not an end in itself; a legal contrivance which individuals have discovered to advance their interests in a world of uncertainty. Indeed, its purpose in some important respects can only be established by reference to the purposes of those who manage and own it. Since, as I suggested earlier, the corporation only exists because of the absence of perfect competition, it must be understood primarily in economic terms. In a world of uncertainty the success of the corporation depends upon the skill and ingenuity of its individual members exploiting profitable opportunities.

Only if corporations behaved in a regular and predictable manner, and every agent fulfilled a specified and unchanging function, could it be plausibly said that it displayed a group cohesiveness equivalent to biological person-hood (and even then this depiction would be little more than a metaphor). But in fact a great deal of entrepreneurship goes on in corporations, and this is the phenomenon of identifiable individuals responding to changes in the environment and displaying that alertness to new opportunities in the inevi-table flux of economic life. If these known individuals are to be rewarded for their contributions to the success of the enterprise then surely they are equally responsible for its moral (and other) failings. There is a compelling moral symmetry here. Sometimes it may be difficult to disentangle individual efforts in necessarily collaborative activities but the exposure of a practical problem is not the same thing as demonstrating some metaphysical truth.

From this it follows that guilt for criminal wrong-doing should properly be attributed to the individuals directly concerned. Indeed, those business ethicists who insist on corporate criminal liability also claim that both indi-viduals and the corporation should be prosecuted for crimes. In fact, the issue was confused in the Ford Pinto case because none of the executives who were culpable was put in the dock. This has not happened since (in the Boeing case, a separate charge of theft was brought against the person who actually committed the offence). It is the case in English law that the 'directing mind(s)' of the corporation have to be identified and convicted before a criminal charge against the company can succeed. And these individuals must be very closely connected with the criminal act itself.

The desire to go beyond individual actions in the kinds of horrific events that lead to corporate manslaughter charges is understandable. Civil actions, no matter how costly they may turn out to be, seem superficially inadequate an expression of the revulsion that people obviously feel at these, sometimes avoidable, distressing events. It is because the criminal law has an 'expressive function', that is, it indicates strongly society's disapproval of certain actions, that the desire to 'punish' corporations should be so prevalent.

None of these observations justifies the claim that a corporation is a 'person' which exists, for moral purposes and for the punishment of the criminal law, apart from the actions of individuals. Of course, corporate executives may often find themselves in difficult positions, circumstances in which 'loyalty' to the company might compete with the constraints of ordi-nary commonsense morality, but such dilemmas are not solved by shifting responsibility to, or sharing it with, an artificial (if not quite 'fictitious') agency. Surely those Ford executives should have resigned and 'blown the whistle' on the company for the manufacture of the Pinto. Indeed, evidence was readily available of the morally crude calculations that were made of costs of civil actions if crashes were to occur compared to the production losses if the fault were to be corrected. But these calculations were made by individuals.

Presumably, the logical implication of the argument that corporations can be liable for serious criminal offences is that Boards of Directors should be imprisoned, even if they were not immediately involved in the reckless or other behaviour that caused the catastrophe. That would be plausible if individual board members could be shown to be responsible by the normal processes of the criminal law. But in the Zeebrugge case, for example, the catastrophe was caused by the irresponsible action (actually, inaction[28]) of the bosun and his immediate supervisor who both failed to comply with company procedures. It may be the case that, in this and other similar tragedies, the procedures were inadequate. Again, is this not a problem of locating responsibility in particular officers, difficult though that may be? If the corporation is to be charged in addition to identifiable individual wrong-doers then the consequences can, logically, only be massive fines. These are ultimately paid by the owners (shareholders) who had nothing to do with the original offence.

It is also important to note that in the Zeebrugge case the judge specifically refused to allow the whole range of individual wrongs to be aggregated so as to constitute a corporate wrong. This of course makes the crime of corporate manslaughter extraordinarily difficult to prove in law. What is the point of bringing this type of charge against a corporation if it really is the case that only an individual can commit it?

The morality of corporate responsibility for crime is as confused and indeterminate as is the law. Sometimes it consists of a certain kind of utilitarianism: that the threat of criminal sanctions is the only way of ensuring that the constant monitoring of activities, which is required for the avoidance of tragedies, actually takes place. It is assumed here that civil actions for damages, to which nobody could object, are inadequate. Yet utilitarian considerations could point in a different direction: it is plausible to suppose that corporate enterprise would be seriously deterred if boards were criminally and collectively responsible for every wrongful action committed by subordinates. In advance of more convincing moral argument, it is tempting to assume that current pressure for the criminal prosecution of corporations for actions normally thought possible only of biological persons is motivated by 'vengeance' rather than by justice. It is an attitude no doubt strengthened by the low esteem in which the corporation is held (especially in American society).

The last point, of course, is not relevant to the theoretical issue of corporate personality. Despite the failure of the prosecution of the P & O Company in the Zeebrugge case (it could not be proved that its procedures constituted an 'obvious' risk) the possibility of corporate liability for serious criminal action was accepted in principle and this runs counter to the principal-agent theory of the corporation. For while that theory can accommodate the idea that the principals (the owners) should shoulder the burdens of civil liability (indeed, it may encourage investors to be more active in the monitoring of the companies they own) it is difficult to see what kind of theory could convincingly establish the guilt of a collective institution which is required for cases involving criminal intent.

The argument that without the invocation of a corporate mind (embodied in the Board of Directors) crimes would go unpunished because of the difficulty of establishing individual responsibility is unpersuasive on two grounds. First, this practical difficulty is not, surely, the same thing as theoretically establishing the case for corporate criminal liability. If that were the argument then particular persons (board members taken collectively) would be 'used' as means to advance some particular end. The end (safety) itself is obviously good but it is at least plausible to suggest that this could be advanced without the potentiality of rights-violation that the invocation of corporate criminal liability involves. Perhaps the judge in the Zeebrugge case had this in mind when he refused to allow individual wrongful acts to be 'aggregated' so as to produce a collective wrong. Also, he did not dismiss the case against the culpable individuals involved in the tragedy (although the prosecution did not proceed against them).

Second, I wonder how difficult it really is to establish individual responsibility? In most of the standard cases in the US, and all of them in Britain, individuals are charged along with the company. Most theorists of corporate criminal liability admit that the actions of a corporate person have to be activated by biological persons. If this is so, then it is surely in principle possible to identify individual agents in human tragedies.

3   Morality, Markets and Insider Trading

It is in the area of finance that the problems of business ethics have received their greatest publicity. The investment market presents special opportunities for greed to manifest itself and recent spectacular scandals on both sides of the Atlantic have lent a superficial credence to the popular image of financial markets as the source of all that is most venal about capitalism. The rewards that are sometimes earned by successful speculators are almost always condemnable, even if they are achieved in an entirely scrupulous way (as prescribed by both law and conventional morality), because their very vastness offends against popular conceptions of distributive or social justice. These almost always relate factor reward to 'desert' or 'merit' or some supposed notion of objective need. Even Donald Trump, somewhat egregiously said, of Michael Milken's 1987 $550 million salary: 'You can be happy on a lot less money'! The utilitarian appeals to socially beneficial effects of self-interest are rarely persuasive.

Nevertheless, the question of the overall distribution of income and wealth has no relevance to business ethics. It does, of course, concern government: and the injunctions issued to that institution derive from more general social and political philosophy. However, neither 'business' (nor its agents) is responsible for the particular configuration of income and wealth that emerges from a market process and it is simply a mistake to charge business with the responsibility of ensuring, say, a 'Rawlsian' distribution of income, as some American business ethicists have urged.[1] Also, it is a possibility that the recent prosecutions of individuals in the US for breaches of procedural rules may have been really motivated by the fact of their vast earnings. It looks as if the assumption is that to earn a significant amount of money a person must have broken a rule (although that is obviously not necessarily so). It is thus sometimes very hard to disentangle claims of procedural rule violations from complaints about particular individual earnings being in breach of popular theories of distributive justice.

Business ethics nevertheless *is* concerned with moral behaviour under procedural rules in financial markets precisely because of the opportunities that high finance presents for immoral, and often undetectable, conduct. It is in this area that the case for an arm's length morality looks least sustainable, where the gap between justice and utility appears to be the widest, and where the claims of individual autonomy and responsibility for action the least plausible. The last point is especially important since the current desire in Britain to widen share ownership may very well be thwarted by the fact that the complexity of stock market dealings, and the opportunities it presents for the exploitation of the ignorant and vulnerable, is likely to deter people from participation. The all-encompassing moral claim of the principle of *caveat emptor* looks less persuasive in the relationship between skilled financial dealers and ignorant clients than it does between shopkeeper and customer. It is perhaps this practical reason, rather than any theoretical consideration, which has fuelled the demands for tougher regulation of the securities markets, and for greater investor protection.

In two areas at least behaviour in the securities market has provoked hostile criticism: insider dealing and certain actions taken in the often bruising takeover battles that were recorded throughout the 1980s on Wall Street and in the City of London. Insider dealing involves the use of undisclosed information by individuals (usually company employees) to gain an 'unfair' advantage in the securities market: it is conventionally thought to be immoral, though nobody quite knows why. In takeover battles competitors for the 'target' company have been accused of all sorts of deceptions in the struggle for corporate control: most often, rigging the price of shares where the takeover is by the exchange of stock rather than by cash purchase (this is what the Guinness scandal was all about).

Although insider dealing and takeovers usually involve different ethical issues, they have a number of common features which have interested business ethicists. They both involve the vexed question of 'victimless crimes': sometimes questionable behaviour is excused by the claim that nobody is harmed by it. They raise the question of what 'equality' means in the procedural sense. Does justice or fairness in the market for corporate control mean that a 'level playing field' must be guaranteed in which all contingent advantages are eradicated so that the winner really is the best or most deserving (whatever these terms may mean)?

Both phenomena raise again the potential conflict between justice and utility. The stock market's function is to allocate capital to its most productive uses; a process from which (almost?) everybody gains. Does it matter that some minor breach of a possibly disputed rule of justice occurs in this allocative process? This point is especially important as the attempts to correct alleged injustices often hinder the allocative process. Furthermore, it could be that arm's length morality is stretched to the limit in financial markets because of the fact that dealing normally takes place between anonymous strangers : in such relationships there are few 'communal' obligations that can restrain greed. Yet the securities market does depend upon a certain type of trust which the motive of self-interest is said to threaten. This is what is presumably meant by critics who claim that the 'integrity' of the market is damaged by dubious practices, even when no one can be shown to be harmed by them, and when they are not technically illegal.

However, overriding all these moral considerations is the crucial role played by information. In a perfect market, where information is costlessly available to all traders, there would be no ethical problem of, for example, insider dealing since the capital market would instantaneously allocate resources to their most productive uses and there would be no opportunity for any one person to profit from his possession of scarce knowledge. If this is what is meant by a 'level playing field' it is clearly absurd because in the real world there is always scarcity of information and inequality of access to it. The economic relevance of it is a matter of the subjective opinion of traders and hence the exercise of entrepreneurial skills (even those in possession of inside knowledge make predictions about share price movements which could turn out to be wrong). No, the real ethical questions are: who is entitled to the knowledge from which profit may be secured? What agreements between individuals ought to govern the legitimate use of that knowledge? What moral rules should govern the revelation or concealment of vital information in order to prevent harm?

Overall, there is the issue as to whether traditional common law rules (and their attendant morality) are sufficient to secure justice or whether the state through additional criminal and civil law ought to act so as to set some more desirable set of rules. Traditional moral rules are primarily but not exclusively utilitarian, for they are necessary not only for the efficiency of the market but also to secure fair treatment of traders. Thus statutory interventions normally have some deontological basis: they would appear to be inspired by conventional notions of justice, and the implication is that they are to be pursued even at the cost of efficiency. They are not limited to the elimination of harm (in the sense used by Adam Smith).

Sometimes the ethical problems of insider dealing and takeovers run together. For example, a potential bidder for a company will not want his plans to be revealed because this will push up the price of shares in the target company; so perhaps making the takeover more costly than it need be. It is imperative that those involved, primarily the employees of the investment bank handling the deal, refrain from disclosing the information. To disclose information for personal gain would clearly be a breach of fiduciary duty (and, in effect, theft since the employees do not own the information) and does not raise any serious moral issues. This was, in fact, pertinent to the Boesky case. Boesky, a Wall Street arbitrageur, bought information about takeovers from Denis Levine, an employee of various New York investment banks, and traded, to enormous profit, in the shares of target companies.[2] However, questions about the rightful ownership of property and the extent of the fiduciary duties of employees, are themselves complex and raise moral as well as legal issues.

What is insider dealing?

Insider dealing is trading in securities on the basis of information which has not been disclosed to the public. The classic example is still the Texas Gulf Sulphur case in the US in the 1960s.[3] It illustrates nicely the economic and ethical issues involved. Texas Gulf Sulphur was a none too successful company that was searching for mineral deposits in Canada. In April 1964 the market was agog with rumours about an impending discovery of great value. Two company statements were issued, the first was non-committal about the prospects while the second disclosed the true extent of the extremely valuable discovery. Between the two announcements senior employees (and others) bought Texas Gulf stock heavily and hence profited greatly on its price rise following the second announcement. They were convicted in 1968 of insider dealing under Section 10b-5 of the 1934 Securities and Exchange Act which was designed to eliminate unfair practices in securities markets. It is under this rule, the point of which is to prevent supra-competitive returns to investors, that later prosecutions have proceeded; prosecutions which have gradually widened the net of insider dealing.[4] In the US the penalties are both criminal and civil. Before 1984 the guilty were made to disgorge their profits but in Congressional legislation of that year fines of up to three times the value of the profits were imposed in addition to the disgorgement (as well as further criminal sanctions). In Britain, insider dealing was made a criminal offence in the Companies Act (1980) and consolidated in the Company Securities (Insider Dealing) Act of 1985. In Britain statute law does not permit a civil suit against an insider.

Before looking at the purely ethical issues raised by insider dealing it is worth noting an initial difficulty: who exactly are insider dealers? Many people can profit from privileged information: not just direct company employees but stockbrokers, bankers, investment advisers, financial consultants and even spouses and lovers of people involved in the securities market. This raises problems for the rule of law, because such is the discretion granted to regulatory bodies, especially the Securities and Exchange Commission in the US (created under the 1934 legislation) that people cannot know in advance what is or is not undisclosed information or who is entitled to use it. The Supreme Court in the US has tended to uphold convictions of people who are in a fiduciary relationship, i.e. relationships which create legal duties of confidentiality which may extend beyond a formal contract. But the extent of such relationships is vague and imprecise, and it depends very much on the (possible) vagaries of case law. The sins of Levine and Boesky were clear enough but other examples are much less conclusive.[5]

The most controversial example in the US did not involve trading on insider knowledge at all. R Foster Winans, a *Wall Street Journal* reporter who wrote the influential column, 'Heard on the Street', traded in stocks which he tipped and made money, not on the basis of inside information, but on the mere fact that their prices rose *because* he had recommended them (a practice known as 'scalping'). Yet he was convicted in 1985 under the insider trading legislation, and his conviction was upheld by the Supreme Court. The threats to the rule of law and freedom of speech in cases like this have been noted by critics of the current action against alleged illicit stock market practices.[6] The legal and moral confusion in the US arises from the fact that although insider trading was not itself banned by the 1934 legislation, various practices, including trading on privileged information, were made illegal by case law. Winans, for example, was accused of misappropriating information properly belonging to the *Wall Street Journal*. The newspaper itself was content simply to dismiss him but the US Attorney's office brought the case.

The Rights and Wrongs of Insider Trading

The problem (if there is one) is a perfect example of the possible conflict between arm's length morality and the more extensive moral constraints implied in a deontological ethics. We have noted on previous pages that all forms of market trading ought to be conducted according to certain rules, irrespective of, and sometimes in conflict with, utilitarian considerations. The French, in fact, use the expression '*les principes déontologiques*' to describe the ground rules of the financial market. Only the purest Mandevillian would not care about these principles as long as *in aggregate* the system met certain efficiency goals. The deontological rules are rather vague but they normally encompass such moral principles as equality of opportunity and a notion of individuality which requires that persons be treated as ends in themselves rather than as means to the ends of others. This latter ethical injunction is particularly relevant to insider dealing because opponents of the practice could plausibly maintain that company employees (and others connected to them) 'use' outside shareholders precisely in this way. Further, important ground rules are needed in order to allocate property rights in a commercial society. But these are likely to be highly contested in markets where intangibles such as 'information' are traded.

Now it is not true that arm's length morality ignores moral constraints in favour of the utility-maximising imperative. It is just that the constraints are weaker than those that operate in families or in face-to-face small communities. At most it rejects a crude utilitarianism which might sanction a morally dubious action which involved minor losses to some individuals as long as in aggregate the community was in some sense better off as a result of it. Arm's length morality puts a general prohibition on harm (and to that extent bears a resemblance to the Pareto principle of welfare economics). The proponents of insider trading have to argue, then, that the activity is not only generally socially beneficial but also that nobody is harmed by it (it would then be consistent with allocative efficiency in the technical sense). In all other respects, market traders can be treated as strangers and the particular distributive pattern that emerges from such trading is a matter of indifference.

The economic arguments in favour of the decriminalisation of insider trading are relatively straightforward. To be efficient the capital market, like other markets, has to absorb information as quickly as possible. It also has to provide incentives for people to reveal that information: this is why it is claimed that the profits from insider dealing are said to be socially efficient. Only when the information is absorbed can the value of a company be known. This knowledge is contained in its share price and to the extent that transactors trade on more or less correct prices there are no misallocations. In the absence of perfect information, the market performs the function of transmitting ever-changing data; this is, of course, how profits and losses are made. It is very important, then, to know as many of the relevant facts about a company's prospects as possible; announcements of government policy (especially towards takeovers[7]) or any other data that emerge from the economic environment that affect the share performance of the company will be crucial. Research is, of course, going on all the time by investment analysts, but usually the knowledge obtained by this does not compare to undisclosed information in terms of economic value.

Economists argue that an efficient capital market is characterised by a 'random walk' effect, i.e. if all correct information has been absorbed then no one person can predict exactly whether he would be benefited or harmed by changes in prices. If a non-random walk exists then at least one person with prior information can make more or less precise predictions about future price movements. The faster and more freely information circulates the more accurate share prices will be: hence the more likely the existence of a random walk. It is maintained by economists, especially in the pioneering work of Henry Manne,[8] that rules against insider trading (for example, those which were used in the Texas Gulf Sulphur case) impede the flow of information and hence reduce efficiency from which everybody, taken as an aggregate, loses.

But, it may be protested, the speed at which information is absorbed can never be fast enough for prices to reflect correct values instantaneously. The person who buys shares first on receipt of good news will make a gain (and vice versa, he who sells first because he possesses bad news will avoid a loss) and this is likely to be a company employee or someone else with access to the privileged information. The anonymity of the exchange system, it is claimed, cannot mitigate the inequality of information that is a feature of capital markets. It is this anonymity which creates the problem, if there is one, because anyone harmed by insider trading cannot be identified: a feature which is not true of the face-to-face relationship. If any people 'lose' from insider trading it is the market makers, who deal first.

In the accepted sense of the word 'harm', however, it is hard to see how the outsider who sells early has been injured. Of course, he would like to make more money, and he would certainly have done so if he had held on to his shares in the event of a price rise, but the failure to make as much money as possible is not the same as being in a worse position because of someone else's action. The same reasoning applies in the case of a price fall. There is no way of knowing why a person wants to sell (he may need the money) and so we cannot say that he would behave differently in the presence or absence of insider trading rules. An outsider would have sold his shares to anyone so that it is difficult to classify the relationship as one involving an identifiable criminal and an identifiable victim. Again, it is not the direct actions of insider dealers that cause an outsider to take a loss when prices fall but the absence of information. In cases of both gains and losses, the insider dealer is performing the valuable function of pushing prices in the right direction. So far from being 'victims', outsiders normally gain from the generally beneficial effects of insiders supplying information to the market.

However, even Manne admits the theoretical possibility of some unknown person(s) being injured by insider trading. In his *Insider Dealing and the Stock Market*, he writes: 'to the extent that insider trading does in certain circumstances injure some particular individuals, unidentifiable in advance, financial advantages flowing to all shareholders more than compensates for this loss.'[9] He repeats this, in a slightly softened form, in later works.[10] This is a little mysterious but, from the tenor of his writings, it can only mean that the unknown person is 'injured' only in the sense of not making as much money as he might have done. This is clearly the hypothetical first person who sells to the insider who has privileged information. Thus, it is perhaps implausible to say that an outside shareholder has been 'used', in the classical deontological sense, only as a means to the ends of another because we cannot know who he is. The stock market is a venue in which individuals meet as strangers and, provided there is no fraud or deliberate misrepresentation, their transactions are fair despite the fact that there are inequalities of knowledge.

The problem with the argument that compulsory disclosure protects investors is that perfect disclosure is impossible; there will always be some people who get hold of information first. That this must be so is a consequence of the fact that real world markets are not perfectly competitive but are active processes through which knowledge is constantly being revealed. The insider trader has every incentive to disclose his information at some point since this is how he makes his profit. It cannot be assumed *a priori* that disclosure rules will be any quicker at revealing information than normal market processes. In fact, as Manne points out,[11] the problem with legally enforced prohibitions on insider trading is that they cannot be fully enforced. This means that illegal trading on disclosed information will be all the more profitable for the unscrupulous who break the rules.

There is one further argument, again drawn from Manne,[12] that deals a devastating blow to the case for prohibition. What about the case where a person (be he a genuine insider or someone connected to the relevant company) who, having earlier decided to sell, changes his mind on hearing later, quite legitimately, some good news and decides not to sell. In this example, the person secures his profit by *not* trading on privileged information: but the law only forbids actual trading. However, the moral features of trading and not trading on undisclosed information are identical. For all its zeal in tracking down offenders, and in widening the category of insiders to include people who are really outsiders, it is inconceivable that the SEC in America and equivalent bodies in Britain should try to monitor decisions not to trade. Yet would not a strict deontological objection to insider trading imply that they should?

Insider Trading, Entrepreneurship and Property

However, the moral criticism of insider trading is not exhausted by the question of harm to individuals: in fact, most critics now stress this less. There are other deontological principles that are held against the practice: they relate to the question of property ownership, the nature of fiduciary duties that hold in commerce and the problem of equality of opportunity to acquire information. These principles do not as such tell against the 'arbitrary' distributions of wealth that emerge from insider dealing or the harm that practice is alleged to cause. Rather, the argument is that insider dealers are not entitled to their riches because they have traded on information to which they have no moral claim or that they have breached some trust. Thus no matter how 'efficient' (in an economic sense) insider dealing is, it would still be condemnable for its violation of property rights or the breaches of duty it might entail (or both).

The point is illustrated rather well in the notorious Denis Levine and Ivan Boesky cases.[13] Levine was employed by various Wall Street investment banks specialising in acquisitions and mergers. Boesky was an arbitrageur dealing in the shares of companies that were possible targets for takeovers. Levine, abusing his privileged position, supplied Boesky with vital information. From a moral and legal point of view, Levine was a thief and Boesky a fence, as one commentator put it.[14]

In general, however, it is not easy to demonstrate conclusively rightful ownership of property in information, or the extent of fiduciary duties (indeed much of the criticism of the SEC's activities is directed towards its attempts to widen the scope of the fiduciary duty not to trade on privileged information way beyond the immediate employees of companies). It is unlikely that positive law can settle these issues since, for jurisprudential reasons, a fixed code will not be able to encapsulate in words all the complexities, for example, of property. In the absence of firm statutory guidance, courts inevitably invoke common standards of fairness in upholding claims to property.

Those who condemn insider dealing often claim that it does breach property rights because the legal owners of a company (the shareholders) are entitled to *all* the gains from the use of their assets: the employees are entitled only to salaries, bonuses and other emoluments that are specified in the employment contract. Thus the gains from insider dealings are not entrepreneurial profits but theft. Although it is always logically possible for employment contracts to be written so as to exclude insider dealing, examples are rare. All the major prosecutions for insider dealing derive from interpretations of statute (the original 1934 Act in America and the 1980 law in Britain). There are, however, at least two powerful arguments to show that the practice is not condemnable (they are additional to the standard arguments from the desirability of the fast flow of information which is required for the economic valuation of companies). They both derive from a theory of entrepreneurship and the just acquisition of property. One is not strictly a moral argument since it refers primarily to the utilitarian advantages that accrue from entrepreneurship within the firm. The other is more ethically ambitious because it tries to show that insiders are actually entitled to at least some of the extra value that their activities create. Both, however, have their intellectual roots in Austrian economics.

Austrian Economics, Markets and Property

Very briefly, Austrian economics starts from the (surely plausible) assumption that market economies are never in equilibrium but, at the most, show a tendency towards equilibrium: a tendency which is brought about by agents following price signals (information) transmitted by the market. If there were equilibrium states of perfect efficiency, when all prices are correct, then these outcomes could simply be commanded. However, because of dispersed information and the fact that real world markets are always in flux, with no economic 'facts' constantly replicating themselves, it is argued that economists should pay more attention to the mechanisms that determine the market process itself. I have already shown that the phenomenon of market process gives rise to some of the ethical problems associated with business. At the purely economic level, it is the mechanism of entrepreneurship that is crucial: for that is the human capacity to spot gaps in the markets and price differentials which can be exploited so that 'profit' is obtained. Without the possibility of entrepreneurial profit, an economy will not be pushed towards efficiency, and everybody will be worse off in a welfare sense.

The relevance of this to the insider trading problem is that, because of the nature of modern business organisation, with its large-scale corporations and the division between ownership and control, entrepreneurship may only be possible within the firm when there are opportunities for employees to gain (over and above their normal emoluments) through the exploitation of undisclosed information. Human actors need motivation to seek out new information, to innovate and to perform all the economic functions necessary for the efficient use of resources. Without the opportunities for profit large organisations may atrophy and those grim prognostications of the decline of capitalism into routinised production may be realised. Indeed, Galbraith and other critics of the large-scale corporation say its profits come from monopoly power rather than genuine entrepreneurship. Proponents of insider dealing are, in effect, saying that without the practice corporations might end up just as Galbraith suggested (despite the obvious economic and ideological differences between his view and that of the market school).

Insider dealing is then recommended as a way of motivating personnel to galvanise corporations; owners will in fact gain because as outside shareholders the value of their assets will rise. The standard objection to this view is that if insiders are allowed profits from dealing on undisclosed information then this in turn might send out the wrong signals. They might be encouraged to spend more time in share dealing than on working for the company. They might also have an incentive to circulate false information. All this seems difficult to sustain. It ignores the filtering-out process of the market. Active shareholders would soon discover if employees behave in this way and take appropriate action. The argument depends very much on the implausible claim that the division between ownership and control renders shareholders powerless in the face of invulnerable managements.

However persuasive the entrepreneurial argument may be in an uncomplicated utilitarian sense, it still leaves a moral gap. Of course, positivists in ethics do not mind about this; or at most claim that moral arguments are simply inconclusive. Manne is particularly scathing towards those writers who bring normative arguments to bear on insider trading. He writes that: 'the discovery of ethical and moral issues and a recurrent insistence on this approach strike me more as an outgrowth of frustration than of cogent analysis.'[16] However, people do expect utility-maximising actions to be consistent with a wider morality and many insist that in a pluralistic world it would not be irrational to trade some utility for the maintenance of the integrity of a moral principle. That is why all financial systems and business organisations have moral codes. Even Manne's insistence on the absence of injury (despite the mysterious minor qualifications that he makes to this statement) from insider trading is an implicit but important concession to the moral view.

It is vital, then, to establish that the fruits of insider dealing do fall to the 'right' people and that these persons are not identified merely as abstract agents necessary for economic co-ordination, but are concrete individuals whose moral entitlements are demonstrably legitimate. Only a theory of property rights can, in this context and others, unite utility and morality. If shareholders own the information on which an insider trades then they are entitled to some of the gains which accrue from the use to which it is put. On the other hand, it could be maintained that the insider is under no obligation to reveal since it is his *guess* that a particular piece of information will be profitable and to make him reveal it (at a time which he would not prefer) would be to deprive him of his (legitimate) entrepreneurial profit. The question then is about the ownership of information.

In traditional classical liberal theory (from John Locke), legitimate property ownership depends upon an agent 'mixing his labour' with previously unowned objects. Although the principles implicit in this criterion of ownership are hedged around with all sorts of qualifications, its main thrust is clear enough: that just proprietorship is a function of the value added to nature by acts of individuals. Although its original application, to land ownership, is of little contemporary relevance, it has acquired a more universal role and can be used to legitimate ownership whenever humans exercise their alertness and capacity in the creation of economic value. Thus entrepreneurship, which is exercised in the rearrangement of the factors of production to more productive uses, or in the spotting of some hitherto unnoticed gap in the market, is said to be a constant feature of free exchange. Production then depends upon some original act of discovery which has its reward in profit.

Israel Kirzner has analysed most systematically the notion of the market as a process of entrepreneurial discovery and, more recently,[17] annexed it to our conventional notion of justice, i.e. that distribution is just which flows from original acts of appropriation and discovery. Kirzner argues that, apart from the most primitive and repetitive production systems, the market is a continual process of discovery, a process which generates profit. The latter is income which is derived from speculating (successfully) on the future value of a discovered object. In essence, it is a reward for the exploitation of ignorance: seeing an opportunity before someone else has noticed it. Economic value does not inhere in physical objects but in the realisation of the uses (profitable) to which they can be put.

The justice of original acquisition and discovery derives from the simple, and intuitively appealing, 'Finders Keepers' rule. Original acts of discovery yield profitable returns which are just if they do not involve fraud or deliberate misrepresentation of the facts. However, the rules of justice do not require that all the information that is relevant to profitable discovery should be revealed: otherwise someone else gets the profit.

In a familiar example: a person may own an old painting which he does not know is a Rembrandt. If someone, realising its true value, buys it for a few pounds, has that person acted unjustly in not revealing his information? Finders Keepers is claimed to be a valid rule of justice because in a free market the profitable opportunity is available to all comers: as long as the agent does not impede others in the pursuit of the opportunity he is entitled to his reward (profit). Thus it is the buyer who 'owns' the knowledge that the painting is a Rembrandt. The owner could always find out. If he consulted an art dealer then the latter would be under a fiduciary duty to reveal the information. In the hypothetical example, the refusal to reveal the fact about the painting is condemnable, but not from a property rights morality. However, and this is relevant to the securities market, there is often a thin borderline between refusal to reveal information and fraud.

In modern productive systems, Kirzner claims, individuals, even at the lowliest levels, are discovering things. Thus, in contrast to the equilibrium theory of factor reward, which relates income to marginal productivity in repetitive, static systems, Kirzner sees it as a just compensation for acts of discovery and innovation. Entrepreneurship goes on within the firm as well as within the economy as a whole. If employees in the corporation are creating value through acts of discovery then the Finders Keepers rule entitles them to the rewards that accrue to their ingenuity: after all, the owners (the shareholders) did not create *this* value. It is, on this view, difficult to see why trading on undisclosed information is theft in the way that appropriating the office stationery or making a personal telephone call are. Other people in the company, including the shareholders, are at liberty to seek out the information which yields a profit. If the argument is a purely moral one, it may not be easy to distinguish genuine acts of discovery out of which value is created from the value created by routine employment. If it is the former then the information produced may be said to belong to the individual discoverer, but if it is the latter then the company may legitimately claim its ownership.

However, this does not constitute a simple knock-down argument in support of the justice of insider trading. For employee-owner relationships are complex and are defined by a set of often vague rules, ranging from strict contracts to imprecise fiduciary duties. At the moral level it is not clear that the anonymity between the two agents is sufficient to validate the profit that is secured because of the ignorance of one of them. One cannot say that a refusal to divulge is unambiguously not fraudulent. The shareholder may not be in a position to find out what is going on in a company and is not therefore able to compete for entrepreneurial profit.[18]

This inequality of access to information is sometimes used as an ethical constraint on insider information: the stock market to be 'fair' requires a level playing field. It could be argued that even under the austere Finders Keepers rule the profits from insider trading are still unjust because insiders have an advantage and reap profits which are not a reward for discovery but are monopolistic rents derived from their privileged position within the company. Note that this argument is not the same as the egalitarian's claim that a level playing field requires that market traders should have equal information. This is clearly an impossibility. The inequality of information that characterises all market exchanges is usually the result of individuals expending time and effort to find out things. The rewards to discovery are not windfall profits (although one can easily think of examples which look very much like this), but the results of using certain skills. As long as individuals differ in their endowments and capacities there will be differential rewards, the elimination of these is not only efficiency reducing but also rights-violating.

The argument for a level playing field does not require egalitarian sentiments but rather it indicates that there might be certain barriers to information which make its acquisition excessively costly or even prohibitive for some. Can shareholders really find out all the relevant facts about, say, ICI's development plans? If this were the argument against insider trading it would have some force; indeed its justification might reduce to a purely utilitarian one. However, it is not normally made in this way but in terms of harm, breach of duty or 'theft' of company property. The gains that accrue to a company employee because he has exclusive access to information could be said to be unjust by a Finders Keepers rule. This rule obviously does not require equality of access but it does require the possibility of acquiring valuable information.

Nevertheless, with regard to the insider trading issue, neither this nor any other principle of prohibition seems to have concerned outsider shareholders and employees (the participants in arm's length relationships in the stock market). For very few companies seem to have voluntarily imposed restrictions on the use of information before this prohibition became a part of positive law.

The Limitations of Limited Justice

One suspects that the *animus* against insider trading reflects the influence of other moral principles than those of fairness and allocative efficiency. In the twentieth century Adam Smith's principle of procedural justice, those strict rules which ought to be legally enforced, has given way to a conception of justice which is as much concerned, if not more so, with the distribution, or more accurately, redistribution, of wealth. Thus although action against insider trading looks as if it is about the rules of fairness, it is surely just as plausible to interpret it as an expression of hostility towards the 'excessive' rewards that go to insiders. No amount of argument to the effect that everybody gains from the faster flow of information that it brings seems to be persuasive against the view that some people get more than they ought. Nevertheless, from the classical liberal point of view, the phrase 'everybody gains' is important: for that philosophy has normally held that appropriation can go on subject to some sort of proviso, such as: 'nobody is made worse off by the action'.[19] The argument that insider trading is Pareto-efficient meets that proviso subject to the minor qualifications mentioned abo ve: though it is silent on the particular distribution that occurs from it.

If the objection is not simply redistributivist it can only be based on some deontological principle other than, or more expansive than, the simple one contained in the basic rules of exchange. No matter how fast the information were to circulate, so that the possibility of supra-competitive gains (and losses) is reduced, the argument holds that since the whole system is ultimately based exclusively on self-interest (or 'greed') it is condemnable. Usually, the principle of the 'integrity of the market' is called into play here: that exchange will lack any moral acceptability if its only animating force is self-interest. It is difficult to give a precise account of such feelings but they are directed against the arm's length view of business morality. The very impersonality of the stock market, it is claimed, is the source of the undermining of those communal duties which are so much emphasised in today's moral climate.

They are not without foundation, although no moral theorist has produced a satisfactory account of what such duties might be. Equally important, however, is the question of how a fully fledged communal ethic can be made consistent with those motivations which have historically been the most effective in the production of prosperity. Still, our moral world is a pluralistic one in which the principles of limited justice and market allocation compete with perhaps more elevated ethical aims. Kirzner,[20] for one, does not deny that there are supererogatory (desirable but not enforceable) duties; and it is these that underlie the dissatisfaction that many people feel at the market's blind, impersonal allocation. The fact that most City (and Wall Street) scandals involve outright fraud, misappropriation of investors' money and various deceptive practices, all of which are obviously condemnable by an arm's length morality, is not enough to assuage the moralists. But business moralists have yet to produce a convincing account of an alternative morality. One suspects that the only genuine meaning that the phrase 'the integrity of the market' can have is that the financial system must maintain standards of probity if small investors are not to be deterred. It can have little to do with motivations because the small investor is spurred by the same impulse as the biggest bond and equity dealer, namely, self-interest.

Sometimes the distinction between fraud and the deliberate refusal to reveal information is hard to make. An investment consultant who advised a person to put his life savings into a company he knew to be in serious trouble would clearly be acting immorally, and quite probably would be in breach of his fiduciary duty. But not all cases are so clear-cut. After all, people invest in the stock market because they expect to make more money than in a building

society account: that necessarily involves risk. (Incidentally, so does investment in a building society during inflationary times: but this is, of course, a
question about the ethics of a government's monetary policy.) There is, then,
a distinction between investor protection against fraud and against loss which
the more enthusiastic business ethicists do not often appreciate.

The fact that laws against insider trading vary in their severity from country
to country suggests that the immorality of the practice is by no means
established. Why, for example, is it not illegal in the futures market in the
US, and only so in rare circumstances in the bond market? At the very least,
the criminalisation of the activity should be questioned by anyone seriously
concerned about civil rights and personal liberty.

4 The Ethics of Takeovers

Information plays a crucial role in takeovers, and the bruising battles that often take place in mergers and acquisitions involve disputed claims to rightful ownership of knowledge. The bulk of insider dealing 'scandals' are about illicit trading in the shares of target companies.[1] Because the value of shares of a company are likely to rise in the event of its takeover, making quick profits possible, the activities of the traders have to be conducted according to complex and sometimes arcane rules. Furthermore, competition between bidders for companies provokes the familiar problems of equality of opportunity and level playing fields that we have noted elsewhere in business ethics. The two greatest 'scandals' in recent years, the Guinness affair and the financial career of the American 'junk bond' dealer, Michael Milken, were about the morality of takeovers. Indeed, rightly or wrongly, the 'merger mania' on Wall Street throughout the 1980s damaged the 'integrity of the market' and fuelled the argument that the financial world was governed by unalloyed greed and dishonesty.

Despite the hysteria surrounding takeovers they clearly have an economic function.[2] A takeover occurs because a company's assets are undervalued on the market and rival bidders think that they can manage them better. Takeovers are the major ways in which inefficient managements can be disciplined; indeed, the existence of corporate raiders is simply one refutation of the claim made by a whole host of anti-capitalist thinkers that the division between ownership and control renders shareholders powerless against managements which are allegedly immune from competition. Indeed, hostile takeovers are methods by which the market filters out some of the moral and quasi-political problems associated with corporations as well as contributing to market efficiency.

There are some important economic arguments about takeovers. They are about the efficiency gains takeovers generate and the possibility of monopoly power emerging, if, through acquisitions, one company controls a large part of the market. They are not the immediate concern here. Suffice it to say that market process theory implies that the rearrangement of assets is a continual part of economic co-ordination and that without that possibility entrepreneurial activity would be seriously inhibited. Some economists, however, have denied that mergers and acquisitions are efficient and have even recommended that they be severely regulated or even prohibited. They claim that predators are after short-term profits and their actions do not contribute to the long-run interests of the companies they acquire. However, this is doubtful; for acquisitions must have an economic rationale or they would not occur. Even the claim that takeovers do not ultimately increase the share price of the company, if it is true, is not decisive: the performance might have been worse without the takeover. A competitive market is surely a better judge of economic success than some hypothetical measure of efficiency, normally drawn from static equilibrium models.

The realisation by corporate raiders that the assets of a company can be more efficiently used is a classic example of Kirzner's 'discovery' process: the increased value of the assets because of a takeover is exactly equivalent to the creation of new property to which the Finders Keepers rule applies. Indeed, one suspects that much of the objection to takeovers is itself derived from an ill-concealed moral principle, i.e. there is something 'wrong' about the profits that derive from manipulating paper assets in comparison to those which accrue from more direct production. Yet it is surely plausible to claim that there is a symmetry between, on the one side, the morality of shareholders' trading their property rights and entrepreneurs being rewarded for their discovery, and on the other the efficiency gains that are brought about when the market delivers its verdict on the proper use of assets.

The moral issues arise in the tactics that are used in takeover battles, for with so much at stake one would expect participants to be tempted to resort to dubious practices. The managements of target companies are to be expected to resist a predator. They have everything to lose, especially their jobs, from the reorganisation that is bound to follow a successful takeover. All sorts of arcane devices have been developed by incumbent managements to ward off what they see as mere predators. Alongside management's self-interest, however, is the duty that they owe the shareholders to secure for them the best deal in the battle for control. A whole range of moral duties on business agents could be produced: they extend down the line to include the obligations owed to low-level employees, some of whom are likely to be adversely affected by plant closures, and normally encompass various duties to affected communities. Many of the latter duties belong to the highly contestable 'social audit' of business discussed earlier.

Also, the shareholders of the target company may behave improperly: at least in a manner which can encourage inefficiency. Some, in a strategic position, may stick out for such a high price for their shares that all of the gains that accrue from entrepreneurial skill may go to them. A lot of the complaints made about the price set for the takeover are derived from a selfish desire to capture the entrepreneur's legitimate profit from discovery. Is the shareholders' action immoral? Such tactics, if successful, might be expected to reduce the incidence of takeovers. Still, they do happen so it cannot be too serious a problem.

Since a takeover battle is highly competitive the concept of a level playing field is relevant to the discussion of the fairness of the contest. To repeat an earlier point: this cannot mean equality of information. Someone who knows something about a target company has an obvious informational advantage and if he were not allowed to exploit it there would be little incentive for economic reorganisation. Surely, fairness in takeovers must refer to the tactics used, not the respective positions, in terms of information possessed by the competitors. Unfairness is most likely to arise when the bidder tries to effect the takeover by a share deal than by a simple cash purchase. For there is a clear temptation for the bidder company to use illegal and immoral methods to raise the price of its shares in order to make the offer more attractive to the target company than rival offers. False markets can be manufactured. Indeed, their creation has been an offence at common law in Britain since the last century.

The Guinness Affair (1986)

The Guinness 'scandal' illustrates nicely the kind of moral (as well as legal) issues involved in takeovers.[3] Guinness (under its chairman, Ernest Saunders) was engaged in a fierce and costly battle with the Argyll Group (led by James Gulliver) for control of Distillers, the Scottish drinks corporation which was badly managed and whose share price did not reflect the underlying (or potential) value of the assets. It was a perfect opportunity for Guinness to create a well-integrated drinks corporation through the acquisition of Distillers and Saunders went for it with a rare zeal, even for takeover battles. However, it is important to note that Guinness only came into the fray (as a white knight) after Argyll had made the original entrepreneurial discovery.

In principle it was a good example of someone seizing an opportunity to create new value (the essence of entrepreneurship). According to Kirzner's theory, the initial noticing of that extra property constitutes a *prima facie* claim to it in justice. The person who is alert to such opportunities is entitled to the income that flows from them according to the Finders Keepers rule, provided that no force or fraud is used in the process. There must be a level playing field, in the very minimal sense of equality of opportunity: which means that the race should be 'open' and that no fraudulent behaviour be condoned (even if those defrauded could be compensated). The original act of entrepreneurship requires, in principle, no resources, only mental awareness of economic gain. Other agents, the owners of capital, provide the resources.

This was where the trouble started. The takeover was to be accomplished by a share swap: Distillers shareholders would exchange their shares for Guinness shares of high value. If the deal was to succeed Guinness shares had to be kept at a high value. Guinness was eventually successful in the battle but the activities of Saunders led to criminal prosecutions against him, and his associates, for organising an illegal share support scheme. Apparently, Saunders had used Guinness money (£25 million), without the permission of the board, to buy up Guinness shares (it is of doubtful legality under English law for a company to purchase its own shares) so that their price was artificially inflated. Saunders' associates were paid success fees (and granted indemnities) for their activities in keeping the price of Guinness shares high.

Saunders and others were eventually convicted of, amongst other things, theft and false accounting. It is interesting to note that the affair was only uncovered because of a tip-off by Ivan Boesky.

Leaving aside the question of positive law, share price manipulation looks straightforwardly dishonest: shareholders in the target company are being deceived about the true value of the stock they are being offered. Yet, one is entitled to ask whether the market itself would not filter out this dishonesty? After all, share price rigging is an extraordinarily risky activity. The extra benefit achieved by gaining control of the company must be great enough to offset the costs of the share support scheme. It clearly was in the Guinness case, but this may not always be so. The more efficient the market is the more costly the operation will be since shareholders will soon become aware if the price of the share they are being offered is not its true price. Still, what is the true price? Shareholders of the target company may claim that they are being cheated by being offered overvalued shares but are they not also demanding an 'unjustified' part (indeed all) of the bidder's entrepreneurial profit? In the Guinness case, the Distillers shareholders were eventually compensated for their losses by the Guinness company.

Overall, one suspects that share support schemes are not likely to be effective in the long run irrespective of the state of the law. Shareholders will eventually become more informed, so eliminating the gains (as economic theory would predict). Nevertheless, such activities, shot through with dishonesty as they are, are certain to do the reputation (in which every transactor has an interest) of the securities market a lot of harm. But this is the ultimate problem of business ethics: the integrity of the market depends on the compliance to moral rules of all agents, not one of whom has any real incentive to be that virtuous (largely because of the feature of anonymity in arm's length relationships). Furthermore, it may take the market a long time to filter out the wrongs.

It is still worth asking who was injured in the Guinness affair (leaving aside the 'integrity of the market' argument). Certainly not Guinness shareholders who saw the value of their stock rise as a result of the takeover. It was probably a better deal for the former shareholders of Distillers who did participate in the eventual entrepreneurial gains, as well as being compensated by Guinness, to the tune of £85 million, for their 'loss' because of the inflated value of Guinness shares. Still, the utilitarian advantages here cannot be decisive if there really was not a level playing field: arm's length morality does specifically require that the rules be fair.

The real complaint came from James Gulliver, whose Argyll Group was denied the entrepreneurial gains from the takeover of Distillers by the activities of Saunders and his associates. In an article in *The Times*,[4] Gulliver explicitly referred to the absence of a level playing field. He claimed that his company had been the first to spot the entrepreneurial opportunity, it did all the research on the economics involved and was then cheated of the rightful gains by the actions of Saunders. Saunders was not entitled to Distillers because he broke the law and breached morality. The fact that a Guinness takeover was probably the best result for all the shareholders is not relevant to all this. To make it so would be to appeal to the crudest version of utilitarianism.

Professor Martin Ricketts[5] has produced a more sophisticated, albeit hypothetical, case for Gulliver: one that is more interesting because it would establish the claims of Argyll to the profits of a takeover on moral grounds because they *spotted* the opportunity first. They were entitled to them by the Finders Keepers rule. Note that this claim would hold in morality even if Saunders had not cheated by breaking positive law; he and his associates were convicted of serious criminal offences including theft and false accounting. In other words, if the Finders Keepers rule is to be consistent with conventional morality (as Kirzner claims) then it is the 'finding' an opportunity that gives the property title, not the 'grasping' of it (Ricketts makes an important distinction, which is absent in Kirzner, between finding and grasping). I am reminded of those frustrating occasions in crowded car parks, where, noticing that a car is about to leave, you wait patiently for its departure only to be beaten to the place by another driver who suddenly appears. He has grasped the place which you discovered and one feels justifiably aggrieved even though his action was lawful.

Is it the case that Argyll was morally entitled to Distillers because the employees had seen the opportunity and therefore created the economic value that was predicted to be created from the acquisition? Ricketts says that it could be argued that Gulliver genuinely found the opportunity, Saunders merely grasped it: and it was this that made his original conduct unethical. Ricketts' argument is clever, largely because it does not make use of the more contestable versions of the principle of the level playing field, but I am not sure that it holds. The creation of the extra value required the consent of the Distillers shareholders, otherwise Gulliver's finding could not be realised, despite all the work that had been done. They, in fact, consented to the Guinness offer and therefore the moral argument does return to the tactics used in that offer. They might have preferred Guinness anyway. But still, Argyll were the victims of grossly unethical and illegal conduct.

Takeovers, Business Morality and the Community

Although 'scandals' of the Guinness type have fuelled much of the public outcry over illegal and alleged unethical practices used in takeover battles, an exposure of wrong-doing in particular cases does not exhaust the morality of the issue. The actions of those convicted in the contest for Distillers were condemnable by ordinary law and morality and hence cannot be used as exemplifications of some general principle directed against the market for corporate control. Such practices are not sufficient to condemn outright all mergers and acquisitions in phenomena which are necessary parts of the market process and hence justifiable on general utilitarian grounds. This rationale, of course, does not exclude those moral constraints which are encapsulated in the rules of the game. In arm's length morality, those rules are minimalist: they are limited to questions about the fair treatment of shareholders and the nature of the tactics employed by the participants. However, criticism of takeovers has incorporated a whole range of other economic and ethical arguments, most of which go way beyond minimalist considerations. Although few writers wish to ban them outright most critics seem to desire to legislate a business ethics which would impose significant restraints on the spontaneous process of corporate restructuring that the market generates.

The debate, however, has been tarnished by colourful but uninformative emotions and visceral attitudes rather than rational responses to an economic activity. Since great wealth is earned in takeovers (increasingly by financial intermediaries, investment banks and their employees, and lawyers) the charge of 'greed' is inevitably and invariably levelled at its recipients. While greed is an epithet frequently used to describe the motivations of agents in all business activity it has a particular resonance when used of behaviour in capital markets. During the merger mania of the 1980s on Wall Street and the City of London, the speculators, arbitrageurs and deal-makers were accused of greed because their activities were said to be governed entirely by self-interest and were in no way directed towards the wider interests of the economy and the community. It was suggested that the reorganisation of corporate life that followed mergers and acquisitions did not enhance the economy and productivity but left many 'victims', including dismissed employees and devastated communities whose livelihoods depended on companies that were arbitrarily closed. Even divorce and family break-ups were said to be a direct consequence of merger mania!

It is difficult to disentangle the arguments that are involved in takeovers; and more difficult still to isolate the purely ethical aspects of the phenomena. Some of the dispute is really about economics and whatever moral rationale it has can only be conventional utilitarianism. From a market perspective takeovers are simply a necessary part of the never-ending process by which inefficient managements are punished. Their occurrence is, in fact, a refutation of the thesis advanced by Gardner and Means, and later Galbraith, that the separation of ownership and control protected the corporation from any kind of discipline. Thus, paradoxically, arguments in favour of restricting takeovers actually are directed against the interests of the shareholder and would, if successful, entrench the much-criticised irresponsible managements.[6]

Nevertheless, the utilitarian case for more or less unrestricted takeovers is embedded in a certain kind of morality, the ethics of Western capitalism in which the actors, motivated by self-interest, are not obliged to take account of the consequences to remote agents of their actions. Although many predators and corporate raiders do take into consideration the interests of all affected parties, this is only a supererogatory moral duty and is therefore not compelling; unlike the rules of the game which are held to be obligatory. Other capitalist systems, notably that of Japan, get by quite well with little or no takeover activity. This might be because the business community there is held together by communal values as well as the commercial imperative, so that each agent is more firmly aware of obligations these values impose than his equivalent in the West. The corporation is therefore much more like a 'family' than it is a simple business unit. It is more likely to be the case that competition, which does exist in Japan, is conducted within differing financial arrangements.[7] Furthermore, economic personnel appear to be engaged in face-to-face relationships where 'tacit' rules and practices predominate over the formalism and anonymity characteristic of the City of London and, especially, Wall Street.

However, in Western capitalist economies an all-encompassing communal morality is clearly absent and it would be pointless, indeed destructive, to attempt to impose artificially an 'alien code' of ethics on social and economic orders which have their own mainsprings of action. The Japanese business culture, with its elements of social well-being as sources of morality, and its apparent moral prohibitions against unalloyed self-interest, is perhaps a benign product of spontaneous evolution but other, and surely more familiar, capitalist economies have emerged in a different way. In basically anonymous societies the absence of a communal ethic means that impersonal rules of law and market processes are the only mechanisms that we have to ensure some kind of harmony between personal self-interest, economic prosperity, and common standards of right conduct.

It is true that the Japanese style of doing business may not only have an ethical culture that many anti-capitalist writers have found attractive but it could also have 'efficiency' advantages over the practices of the West. This possibility is apparent in takeovers, which involve considerable resource costs. Investment bankers, lawyers and other intermediaries earn vast fees from what many moralists consider to be a largely unproductive activity. Certainly, Japanese society, with its reliance on informal bonds of loyalty, and non-legalised notions of trust and honour, precludes the excessive use of law in business relationships. But it is worth asking the question: how could diverse, pluralist and anonymous societies, such as the United States, work efficiently were it not for the relative certainty provided by law?

Takeovers and the Public Interest

If the threat of takeover is the only method that market societies have for the attainment of efficiency and the protection of the legitimate interests of shareholders, why has 'merger mania' aroused such hostility? I suspect that the answer to this question lies in the deeply entrenched belief (a conviction as old as capitalism itself) that unregulated markets (especially the market for corporate control) produce a disjuncture between private and public interests: that the motivations of the participants are unlikely to produce benefits for all those affected by the actions to which they give rise. It is this claim that lies at the heart of the argument that corporate raiders and pred-ators are driven by greed. It is the duty of regulators to restrain this impulse on behalf of a collective good that exists independently of the interests of market transactors.

It is not true, of course, that the market society has no underlying conception of the public interest, no notion of a state of affairs from which, in some sense or other, all individuals benefit.[8] It is the case, however, that this is a minimalist conception of the general good that derives whatever value it has from the implausible and impractical nature of the suggested alternatives. All of these invariably involve the advancement of the interests of particular groups, normally those that have influence over legislation: indeed, excessive regulation of takeovers must tend to advance the interests of existing managements.

This minimalist conception of the public interest is a variant of the anonymity of Western business society; for although certain groups do suffer from the relentless reallocation of resources that it produces these cannot be known in advance of the process itself. Its benefits and disbenefits go to unknowable agents: the 'public', which consists of non-assignable individuals, benefits from the continuation of competition which, although on some occasions may disbenefit some, is likely to advantage any one person taken at random.[9] The major virtue of this negative approach to the ethics of the public interest is that it does not depend on the (surely unreliable) demonstration of a substantive and knowable public interest, i.e. one defined in terms of particular commercial arrangements. There is simply no account of the public interest, beyond a common set of rules and practices, which can secure universal support.

This is recognised in British law on mergers and acquisitions: it requires only that a proposed merger be not against the public interest and does not demand that the public good is positively advanced by it. Implicit here is the rather modest claim that the public interest in commercial society is simply the maintenance of the competitive process itself (though, of course, purists would no doubt cavil at those restrictions on takeovers which are derived from a not uncontroversial theory of monopoly). Yet critics often argue that mergers and acquisitions are only acceptable if they actually advance the public interest in some non-minimalist sense. It is difficult to see what this demand can amount to, except a claim for the protection of partial interests which may be disbenefited by merger activity.

The criticism of hostile takeovers and the demand that traders should take into account other interests than those of the shareholders is really a variant of the social responsibility of corporations argument. In the literature,[10] the term shareholder is replaced by 'stakeholder'; which is meant to indicate that other agents as well as holders of stock have an interest in the performance of a corporation. They include employees as well as owners, the community in which the firm is located and sometimes the whole country (as when 'foreign' buyers are resisted on the nebulous ground that their ownership of a 'national asset' would be detrimental to independence).[11] The most familiar complaint is that mergers and acquisitions represent 'short-termism', i.e. the relentless pursuit of profit at the cost of future well-being.

It is difficult to distinguish ethical from economic and public policy arguments here but it is, nevertheless, plausible to suggest that the market filters out some of the supposed ethical problems. The interests of the community are best served by the efficient use of its assets and it follows that so far from mergers and acquisitions being examples of short-termism they are essential steps in a long-run, and indeed, unending competitive process. Furthermore, the dislocations and unemployment that occur from them are ethically no different from those which occur in other parts of the economy. They only appear to be ethical problems because they are visible, whereas the benefits that accrue are invisible. It is difficult to see how legislation designed to prevent mergers could have any other effect than to protect one part of the community from necessary change at the cost of others: which is itself a breach of the ethical principle of the rule of law. People are made unemployed, and are re-employed every day by the normal processes of the market. How could a law be designed which distinguished between the 'victims' of immoral takeover activity (and gave them special protection), and those who suffer from the apparently acceptable forms of the market? Indeed, the 'victims' of mergers are more likely to be the managements of target companies than the workers: which would explain the former's hostility and frequent resort to defensive tactics of dubious morality.

Any ethical evaluation of mergers must involve a careful understanding of the interests of shareholders and other stakeholders in an enterprise. For if we are concerned with the ethics of business society then our concern must take account of the interests of the property holders in that society. It should be remembered that all members of a capitalist economy have an interest in its progress, even though only a minority may be private shareholders, since the bulk of industry is owned by financial institutions through which individuals' pensions, insurance policies and savings are invested. But leaving this fact aside, it is worth stressing that critics of modern business enterprise cannot have it both ways. They cannot criticise the separation of ownership from control in the modern corporation, lament the decline in shareholder power this is alleged to produce, *and* criticise morally the takeover process. For the latter is the most effective way in which the de facto sovereignty of managements can be resisted.

Public policy issues normally relate to the aforementioned 'short-termism', the apparent preference for immediate profits over the returns from long-term investment projects that merger activity apparently encourages. But in addition, the fact that many takeovers, especially in the US, are achieved through the issue of large amounts of debt (especially in management buy-outs) has been a particular focus of criticism: it is claimed that this cannot be good for a market economy in the long run, that the interests of the aggregate are not advanced by what is claimed to be the purely self-interested actions of financial manipulators.

This is the claim, in effect, that the market does not filter out social problems, that the 'Invisible Hand' does not work without harming significant numbers of people. However, the arguments in much of business ethics often turn questions about the aggregate performance of an economy into questions about the conduct of individual participants. Thus, the existence of the alleged victims of takeovers is said to be a necessary consequence of the actions of individual agents. Corporate raiders and predators, because they are motivated by greed, are said to be morally culpable for the fate of those disbenefited by corporate reorganisation. The impersonal forces of the market, the unintended outcomes of anonymous processes for which no identifiable person can be said to be morally responsible, become personalised in the actions of known agents. This transmogrification can be seen at work in popular films, such as *Wall Street*, and *Roger and Me* (a social satire on General Motors rather than on the financial community) where financiers are represented as villains; but the same *motif* is present in more serious criticisms of the financial world. Here the linchpin of the argument is the claim that the interests of stakeholders (in the broader sense so as to include employees and local communities) are sacrificed to those of the narrow world of stockholders and financiers.

This expansion of the moral community, however, is highly controversial, for it is difficult to see how particular agents can be said to be morally responsible for general outcomes which they did not consciously intend. To make them so responsible would be to make the competitive system unworkable. Furthermore, it would be quite unrealistic to assume that intervention and excessive regulation would necessarily overcome the dislocations that inevitably accompany economic change. Short-termism is just as much a feature of government action as it is of private action: and at least the corrective mechanisms are likely to operate more speedily on the latter. The complaint, then, that the financial system is not serving the long-run needs of industry is not a moral question at all but a highly disputed issue of public economic policy. In fact, there is little direct evidence to support the argument that the existence of financial dealing is a disincentive to investments which yield a return only in the long run.

The genuinely moral questions must relate to the *personal* (and corporate) conduct involved in takeovers. We have already noted the Guinness example which did involve serious issues of crime and immorality. Of course, existing managements are bound to argue that the 'rules of the game' are unfair; indeed the activity does depend upon moral features, trust and probity which are difficult to formulate in strict legal terms even in communities governed by arm's length morality. The inappropriate release of price-sensitive information can do great damage not just to the interested participants in a particular merger but also they affect adversely the financial community itself.

At the moment the rules of the game are embodied in the Code on Takeovers and Mergers and administered by the Takeover Panel.[12] Although they are not rigorously enacted in strict positive law, the City has itself non-statutory means to enforce compliance, and they are relevant to legal cases. The most important ethical goal seems to be the fair treatment of all interested agents. But this is a rather nebulous ideal because the key moral terms, e.g. 'fair treatment' and 'interested parties' are infinitely contestable. Although Distillers' shareholders may be said to have been unfairly treated because they were misled about the 'true' price of the Guinness shares they were offered (they were later compensated) not all cases are so clear-cut. It is not even clear if that example is absolutely uncontroversial.

In fact, the furore that has been created by 'City scandals' and 'Wall Street greed' relates normally to straightforward fraud, complicated though these cases may be. Fraud is so obviously wrong that it hardly raises interesting ethical problems or dilemmas. Nevertheless, ethical pressure has built up to condemn practices which are not illegal though perhaps undesirable. Excessive advertising in some of the spectacular takeover battles in Britain was thought to be particularly blameworthy, and indeed is now restricted, though the rationale for this is obscure since the free flow of information is indispensable for the making of sound judgements in the intense competition that characterises takeover battles.

Some of the defensive tactics ('Greenmail', 'poison pills' and so on[13]) used by managements of target companies are usually not in the interests of shareholders. Thus those who criticise morally the predators on the ground that they are motivated by self-interest should remember that those incumbent managements who resist them are often inspired by the same impulse. Moral argument is not advanced by an exclusive concentration on motivation.

5 The Morality of Wall Street

The publicity that has surrounded financial activities, especially on Wall Street in the 1980s, has generated great controversy over the ethics or lack of them in finance capitalism. In defiance of some well-established economic theories, there has been an almost *a priori* assumption that self-interest (invariably translated as greed) operates against the public interest and that traditional rules against fraud and deceit are inadequate to generate a morally respectable order. This is overlaid by an economically crass bias in favour of production over financial dealings: as if the latter were not an essential part of commercial development (a bogus distinction exploited to the point of naivete in the film *Wall Street*).

It is important to distinguish between crime and ethical misconduct. It is not clear whether the criticisms levelled against the financial world are derived from a belief that crime is more prevalent in high finance than elsewhere in the commercial world, and therefore ought to be pursued more rigorously than it has been hitherto, or whether that world itself requires a special sort of law to enforce ethical standards over and above what may be called the rules of just conduct. The latter view seems to be implicit in some of the arguments against insider dealing; here the claim is made that there ought to be equality of access to information and that a competitive market requires a level playing field. It is a view that depends implicitly upon the view that information is somehow costless.

Both of the above considerations might support an ethical argument to the effect that the securities market requires stricter rules than those contained in ordinary criminal and civil law if procedural justice is to be satisfied. The Securities and Exchange Commission (SEC) in the US has accumulated a vast array of powers to enforce rules of fairness: they include the making of insider dealing both a criminal (though it doesn't bring criminal charges) and civil offence. Congress has enacted tough laws, with heavy penalties, including massive fines and lengthy prison sentences, in order to prescribe a certain kind of financial morality. Together with normal criminal law, the 'financial code' constitutes a complex set of rules under which traders have to operate. Arcane though they might be, inhibiting to free exchange though they sometimes are, and unpredictable in their effect, they are not logically connected with justice in the wider, more substantive sense used by political philosophy. That is, they are not designed to generate some apparently desirable economic outcome, some socially just distribution of income and wealth which might be validated by egalitarian ethics, but only to guarantee fairness.

This might seem uncontroversial except for the fact that much of the moral fervour expended on the Wall Street scandals was powered by a popular revulsion against the vast sums of money earned there. It is not, however, within the remit of regulatory bodies to adjudicate on social justice: indeed, distributive questions do not properly belong to business ethics at all. Nevertheless, one suspects that many people erroneously believe that it is impossible to earn the multi-million dollar Wall Street salaries without breaking the law. On the other hand, it could be maintained that such is the range and technicality of securities rules and regulations that it is impossible to make any money at all without breaching some of them.

The controversy reached its peak with the long-running litigation (both criminal and civil) over the activities of the adventurous Wall Street investment bank, Drexel, Burnham, Lambert, and especially its employee, the 'junk bond' innovator, Michael Milken.[1] The conviction and sentencing in 1990 of Milken was the culmination of a long period during which Wall Street came under critical ethical (as well as legal) scrutiny. The Milken case was particularly controversial because the question of both criminal and moral guilt was from the outset much more complex than the earlier scandals involving Denis Levine and Ivan Boesky. Levine readily admitted to insider dealing offences committed while working in mergers and acquisitions for several Wall Street investment banks and to passing on information to Boesky, the phenomenally successful arbitrageur. Both were convicted (Boesky's conviction was actually the result of a plea bargain that included only one felony count, though he made no real attempt to hide his manifest guilt) and it was their evidence that led to the investigation of Milken's activities.

Although Milken was eventually convicted of six offences in April 1990,[2] again as a result of a plea bargain, and given a harsh prison sentence (ten years) in November 1990, in addition to an earlier punitive fine of $600 million, there was more doubt about his case than some other ones. Doubts which were fuelled by the review of his case in February 1991. Indeed, he still has defenders today. Only at a late stage did he agree to the plea bargain, after protesting his innocence throughout most of the investigation, and questions were raised about the pressure brought on him by the SEC and the prosecuting authorities. In fact, he was investigated largely as a result of information supplied by Boesky, who had an obvious interest in co-operating with the authorities. If the ethics of Wall Street were as bad as its critics maintained then one is entitled to be sceptical about Boesky's honesty in this respect.

The ethical behaviour of the agencies became, in certain quarters at least, as much a cause for concern as that of Milken and Drexel. The offences to which he confessed were not, it is generally agreed, cases of serious fraud but rather technical violations of the securities and tax laws.[3] Insider dealing was not one of the six violations to which Milken pleaded guilty (though it was part of the ninety-eight count indictment which was originally served on him). The one possible exception was his involvement in the Finsbury Fund Ltd deal. Drexel had sold the fund to overseas investors for a one per cent commission. This was to be covered by David Soloman, of Finsbury, paying a fraction of a per cent more than normal for securities that Milken had sold to Finsbury. The crime was the failure to disclose this arrangement to Finsbury's shareholders.

In the later review of his case Judge Kimba Wood, the original sentencing judge, seemed to alter her earlier view of the gravity of Milken's offences.[4] In comparison to Boesky's light sentence of three years for serious wrong-doings, he seemed to have been treated unfairly. Judge Wood suggested that in view of this, Milken might only serve three years. What was also interesting was that she made a rough calculation of the direct harm caused by Milken's wrongdoing (the Finsbury deal). It came to precisely $318,082: a miniscule amount compared to the damage caused by Boesky. Of course, a moral and legal wrong is condemnable irrespective of its extent. However, the moral criticism of Milken was not just about his particular activities and offences but about the ethics of Wall Street in general, about greed, and about the alleged adverse effects on the economy and society at large caused by the particular form of financial restructuring of American business that he had pioneered and perfected.

Given the welter of accusations and counter-accusations in the case, the emotional confusion and moral fog that it created and the sheer complexity that it involved, it is difficult to reach any firm conclusions. It is, however, important to note that it illustrates very well the ethical, economic and legal problems that arise when the business world is regulated by rules that supplement those already contained within the traditional civil and criminal law. These extra rules are largely validated by business ethics, those rules of behaviour which are thought to be binding upon financial agents even though they often run counter to the utility-maximising imperative by which capital markets are powered.

A number of separate, though interconnected, ethical principles and issues should be distinguished in this whole affair. They can be summarised as follows: the economic value and moral character of the activities Milken and others were engaged in; the distributive implications of financial markets; the morality of 'harm'; and the rule of law in securities regulation. In all of these matters there seemed to be an incoherent mixture of utilitarian and deontological principles at work. Critics claimed that what Milken (and others) did was 'bad' for the American economy or, even if it did some good, it was accompanied by such immorality (normally in the form of 'harm' inflicted on innocent people) that no rational, ethical agent could consistently uphold it. The defenders of Wall Street said that not only were the apparent disruptions to and reorganisations of business activity that the new forms of financing developed in the 1980s economically necessary in a utilitarian sense, but that no one was 'harmed' in the process.

The Financial (and Ethical) Career of Michael Milken

Michael Milken has probably become the most controversial financier this century: praised by some for his undoubted flair yet reviled by just as many for his alleged malign effect on the structure of the American economy through burdening it with debt and for apparently pushing ethical standards in financial markets to a new low. Because of the hysteria created by his activites it has been difficult for rational debate over both his economics and morals even to emerge, let alone to be decisively concluded. Yet Milken is by no means a unique figure in American economic history: entrepreneurs have in the past cut through existing commercial structures, offended prevailing business power elites and earned, whether deserved or not, reputations for ruthless, unethical behaviour. Milken effected a revolution in American investment banking equivalent to that achieved by J P Morgan earlier in the century and parallel to the industrial innovators of the past who were castigated as 'robber barons'.

The reason why Milken has suffered even more opprobrium, and has been subjected to even greater economic and moral censure than his predecessors, is that the vast increase in the regulation of securities markets, and the criminalisation of many actions which were hitherto minor civil wrongs, have made it superficially easier for moral criticism to stick. Added to that is the prevailing anti-capitalist ethics of the American intelligentsia: prominent left-liberal spokesmen found it easy to condemn Milken merely because he was spectacularly successful in an 'unjust' system. Leading figures in the business world were equally critical, but for a different reason. Milken was a radical innovator in a conservative world and a threat to their economic power base.

Milken pioneered the (inaptly named) junk bond: it was first used as a method of finance for small and medium sized companies deemed not creditworthy by the orthodox institutions. Only later was it used to enable the hostile raiders (predators) to take control of, and break up in some cases, well established American public corporations. What might be thought of as no more than a regular feature of capitalist development, i.e. the emergence of new financial methods, became the source of all that was wrong in America's economy, i.e. debt, and all that was immoral in American society, i.e. greed.

The junk bond is no more than debt which is of lower quality than that issued by blue chip companies. To the extent that the majority of debt is not rated as investment grade quality by the standard rating agencies then the majority of debt is technically junk. Milken's skill lay in noticing that the default rate on so-called junk was quite low (in fact, he got hold of the idea from a learned and little read treatise by W Braddock Hickman, published in 1958, called *Corporate Bond Quality and Investor Experience*). Since this debt paid higher rates of interest than investment grade bonds there was money to be made if investors spread their funds widely. Even bonds that were close to default could be made to earn profits: they could be bought up cheaply. Another Milken observation was that bankruptcies were much rarer than most people thought so that the risks were less than indicated by the credit rating agencies.

In fact, much of Milken's behaviour is explicable by Austrian political economy. It was his alertness to these inaccuracies in the market's existing valuations that generated the profit. Again, the securities market is not technically 'efficient' in an equilibrium sense, rather it shows a tendency to efficiency when people, such as Milken, speculate successfully on the future. Indeed, one of the methodological problems with the established credit rating agencies was that their estimations of creditworthiness were based on past data. This tends to lead to the overvaluation of blue chip firms and undervaluation of newer enterprises. Yet a sophisticated analysis of a firm's prospects based on future cash flow, an activity in which Milken showed great expertise, proved to be remarkably reliable.

Thus the enormous fees that Milken earned can be justified, as well as explained, in terms of the moral gloss that Kirzner adds to the Austrian theory of entrepreneurship. Although he was employed by Drexel it would be absurd to say that Milken's income was a salary paid because of his physical productivity. His income was largely profit: the reward for genuine acts of discovery. He in effect owned the information (as a form of property) from which he and others derived benefit.

Furthermore, Milken's activities promoted an ideal much praised by Adam Smith (and the absence of which as been frequently commented on by the critics of capitalist enterprise): the governance of industries by owner managers. Through the finance he was able to raise, and his uncanny ability to spot promising enterprises, Milken wrought substantial changes in American industry. By, to some extent, overcoming the distinction between ownership and control, Drexel-financed operations produced a managerial class which had a direct interest in the success of the enterprise. This stood in sharp contrast to the prevailing structure in which managements were likely to be in conflict with stockholders and were anxious to insulate themselves from the pressure that latter would like to bring to bear on them.

This was seen in the much-maligned hostile raids that Drexel-financed predators made on established but inefficiently run companies. Of course, the fact that the assets of a company may be so misused that its share price does not represent its potential value, and hence improvements may be secured by a takeover, is hardly new. What was distinctive about Milken's activities was that they were made possible by his innovative financial methods. The hostile takeover and the highly-leveraged buyout were made possible by the development of the junk bond. In America, takeovers had been made difficult by legislation similar to that which obtains in Britain, that made it obligatory for a raider to announce his bid as soon as he had bought 5% of the equity in the target company. This means that the share price rises so that the takeover becomes more costly. Not only that but conventional banks were reluctant to lend money to hostile bidders. The availability of new forms of debt allowed these impediments to competition and enhanced efficiency to be overcome. Milken was able to finance some of the most famous raiders in recent American history—T Boone Pickens, Carl Icahn and Raymond Perelman amongst others.

This whole process was greatly resented by the corporate establishment who faced real competition for the first time in decades. The raiders were accused of showing no interest in the corporation, its research and development and long-term plans and its workforce but only in acquiring its assets and breaking them up for profit. (It is certainly true that it was possible to borrow money for the raid, sell off parts to pay down the debt and be left with a company at virtually no cost). During the heyday of the junk bond era giant corporations such as Revlon, Phillips Petroleum, Unocal, TWA, National Can, and Union Carbide were attacked, though not all raids were successful. Some of the raiders confounded the critics and eventually became managers themselves, notably Carl Icahn at TWA.

Even though only 10%[5] of Milken's junk bonds were used to finance hostile takeovers they have become the focal point of the criticism of him. Economists disagree in the US as much as in the UK about the merits of this sort of corporate restructuring but a strongly-held view seems to be emerging that the discipline corporate raiders exert on management is necessary for efficiency,[6] even though many critics question the motives, social attitudes and general morality of the predators.

There is more than a trace of Mandeville's *Fable of the Bees* in all this. It will be recalled that in the poem, the bees in their original state were selfish and uncaring yet their indifference to conventional morality in fact resulted in overall happiness. Misery resulted as soon as they tried to be moral. The corporate raiders are the bees and, despite their almost blatant selfishness, the claim is that necessary and socially beneficial consequences ensued. One suspects that the moral motivations that inspire political and legislative attempts to curb the raiders will produce a similar malaise. Mandeville's doctrine was a more brazen version of the theory later sanitized by Adam Smith.

Still, are raiders that immoral? The exchanges between them and the target company's shareholders are free and uncoerced. Indeed, it is the managements that use all sorts of defensive tactics to fight off the raiders who are open to moral censure. For to the extent that they are successful (and they sometimes are through the misuse of shareholders money and because of political lobbying) they undermine the rights of their employers, the owners of the enterprise.

There are circumstances, however, in which the Mandevillian theory does not work out so benificently. I mention as an example, greenmail. Here managements buy back at a premium the shares that a raider has purchased on the understanding that the takeover will not go ahead. This obviously looks like unfair treatment of other shareholders and this author has yet to see a satisfactory economic explanation of the phenomenon. It does not even have the Mandevillian 'virtue' of producing a public benefit out of a private vice since its whole purpose is to prevent the takeover being consummated. One has sympathy with those enraged shareholders who lobbied Congress for the abolition of greenmail. Milken could not have been involved in this (he was not, of course, a raider himself) and T Boone Pickens was resolutely opposed to taking greenmail. But it did happen.

At the macro-level there was a range of reasons why highly leveraged buyouts turned out to be so profitable. There is evidence that the break-ups that did occur were of conglomerates that had diversified far too much and hence undermined their profitability. The classic example is Revlon, which had extended beyond its cosmetics base into health care: Ronald Perelman's divestiture of these units after his takeover made the firm viable. The diversification of the conglomerates had been brought about by conventional financial methods and it was shown often to be in the interests of the existing managements. There were probably few synergies (efficiencies through merger activities) in the prevailing arrangements. Milken and his raiders were upstarts and, paradoxically, ruthlessly egalitarian.

Another fact that made leveraged buyouts attractive is that the payment of interest on corporate debt is tax-deductible whereas dividends on stock is not. Still, this is a matter of government tax policy; it has little to do with business ethics.

Greed

Milken, more than anyone else, was held to be the apothosis of greed. Indeed, in his sentencing hearing, Judge Kimba Wood said that she had been pressed by massive correspondence 'to render a verdict on a decade of greed'.[7] Obviously, the well-publicised details of Milken's income (especially for 1987, when he earned $550 million) were decisive in generating this intense moral pressure. But moral pressure is not ethical argument and a person is not culpable merely because respected opinion-makers (which at the time included almost, but not quite, everybody) say he is. After all, it is still not technically illegal to earn enormous salaries in Western capitalist countries. If it is immoral then perhaps he should have given most of it away (in fact, he did donate large amounts to charity). Earning that kind of money is apparently immoral because it is somehow a result of greed; and greed is seen by most people to be a moral vice.

Or is it? Indeed, what exactly is greed, apart from the name we attach to the attitudes of those who earn more money than we do, or who acquire it by methods, or pursue activities, of which we disapprove? Yet the word greed has no place in the economic vocabulary, for the earnings of labour are simply those that are required to bring that factor into its most productive uses (i.e. those that satisfy the desires of the consumers). It is important to note that the price of those labour services is not set by persons themselves, however greedy they might be, but by the processes of an anonymous market. In a strict sense, distributive questions are irrelevant to the economics of the market, for as long as the factors of production are efficiently employed the economy is at an 'optimum' irrespective of which persons are the major beneficiaries of the allocation and irrespective of their particular moral qualities (especially their supposed 'deservingness'). The standard argument is that if there is some disturbance of the allocative process then an optimum will not be reached and a society will be, in an economic sense, worse off.

Business ethicists might well argue that this method of factor reward lacks any moral validation and indeed it does in the standard formulation: that is why the charge of greed that is levelled at the beneficiaries has such an emotional, if not rational, appeal. Wall Street traders are personalised and therefore vulnerable to such charges whereas the market process is impersonal, dehumanised and scarcely understood: in theory, it has no ethic of entitlement in the accepted sense. However, a theory of property entitlement can be read into it. The bulk of the income earned by specialist traders in the securities market derives from their insight into the future uses to which scarce information can be put. A takeover deal creates new property rights in the value of the reorganisation of assets that it produces. This argument holds independently of the claim that utilitarian benefits accrue from the efficiency gains that such reallocation brings: though the two rationales are not inconsistent.

I stress the former, the property rights argument, because it is fundamentally a distributive one in the moral sense. The more familiar utilitarian rationale for high income is morally inadequate precisely because it deals only with anonymous agents (indeed, this feature has lent some plausibility to the erroneous argument that some other agent, the state, could do the coordination job better than decentralised persons) and makes no judgement about their moral character. The implication of all this is that high earnings are not simply inducements to make an economy work but income to which the recipient is morally entitled by his use of legitimately acquired property.

A more generalised moral theory of distributive earnings in financial markets would have to include both a consideration of the activities of the recipients of income and the purpose of the enterprise in which they are engaged. If business itself is not an immoral activity, and the actions of its agents are not in breach of conventional rules of morality, then it is difficult to say that the income earned is a product of greed.

Since, as I have shown, entrepreneurship promotes the essential purpose of the market, which involves the discovery and exploitation of new opportunities and the creation of new value, the rewards that accrue to it have a justification in distributive justice. They are not 'windfall' gains which require no personal activity at all, but necessary elements in an economic enterprise.

The profits secured from takeovers can be contrasted with those that accrue from, say, arms-dealing and the production of weapons for dictators. For the latter do, in most cases, emanate from greed: an attitude that places personal aggrandisement above all other moral constraint. In many examples the purpose of the activity to which the arms dealer contributes is an immoral one (even though it may not be illegal), and the use of the epithet of greed has a clear applicability. No doubt, critics of junk dealers would maintain that the activity to which it related was immoral. They would claim that it was solely concerned with the manipulation of assets rather than the production of real wealth. This activity, it is claimed, is immoral because it has adverse effects on the community: the earnings that accrue from it are therefore unjust. But, as I have indicated earlier, this has not been demonstrated by the critics of corporate restructuring. Indeed the argument is an economic rather than a moral one and serious debate has been obfuscated by the attribution of undesirable motives to the agents involved in the necessary process of market correction.

The above argument only holds if no harm is committed in the process of wealth accumulation. Greed would have some clear meaning and moral application if it could be shown that other people's rights were violated in order to secure wealth. Someone so obsessed with personal aggrandisement that he was prepared to sacrifice other people's interests for it, indeed use other people merely as a means to his own ends, would be acting immorally (even if those ends themselves are desirable). The problem arises, however, over the meaning of harm. When harm to identifiable agents occurs, no social improvement (in terms of allocative efficiency) can be said to take place. In such a circumstance someone has been made worse off by the action and no matter how great the benefits to everyone else, there has been a technical misallocation. However well the stolen information was used in the Boesky case, it was still stolen information: deontological ethics and Paretian welfare economics were in harmony in condemning his activities.

In the Milken case[8] things were a lot more complex and there were really two accusations that derived from the harm principle. One was quite persuasive: it was claimed (and he formally admitted to the charges) that he had committed certain securities violations and tax avoidance schemes that were technically fraudulent. However, none of the six offences to which he pleaded guilty included the heinous crimes which the more emotional of his critics attributed to him. Even Judge Wood, at the sentencing hearing, said that his actions were only just beyond the margin of legality. Most of his crimes in fact arose out of his rather complaisant attitude towards the illegal activities of others. His defenders claim that he was a somewhat passive co-operator in illegality rather than a direct instigator of it.

Milken's most assiduous critic, Connie Bruck in her *The Predators' Ball*,[9] detailed a whole list of serious illegalities and immoralities committed during his reign. These covered conflicts of interests in his dealings, his attempt to monopolise the junk bond market, suspicious diversion of monies from lenders to himself and Drexel, bringing undue pressure to bear on lenders to invest in junk bonds, and many other venalities. Her book was published before the plea bargains and the eventual settlement of the cases against both Milken and Drexel. It is perhaps more difficult to sustain these allegations now, although her description raised a large number of embarrassing questions about Milken's behaviour.

However, one suspects that the charge of greed would still have been made even if there had been incontrovertibly no wrong doing on his part. It is hard to see how Milken's income would have fallen that much had the admitted offences never occurred. In these circumstances, greed simply means that someone is getting more than they need or deserve. This is, in effect, an egalitarian theory which holds that no efficiency considerations should ever override these familiar moral imperatives. But these are arguments of a broad ethical and political argument and have little to do with business ethics if that subject is to be at all manageable. Indeed, such is the contentious nature of such concepts as need and desert that it would be unwise to make them subjects of business morality.

If one takes a more expansive view of business morality than is traditionally held then no doubt Milken did not live up to the Aristotelian vision of what it means to be a 'virtuous man'. A man who was apparently solely concerned with making money (although he didn't apparently spend much of it on himself) does not present a particularly attractive picture. Again, the Mandevillian lure of business seems to exclude the possibility of making those personal sacrifices, which war and religion require of us, and which the ethical life often enjoins. However, a deontological business ethics does not require commercial agents to strive for the higher life but only that they adhere to strict rule of just conduct. There is enough to do here for businessmen without burdening them with further moral tasks. there is too much disagreement in relatively anonymous societies about what the ultimate good is for that to be a feasible moral goal: for the general population as well as for business agents.

Still, Michael Lewis's witty account of life as a bond trader in New York and London in *Liar's Poker*[10] does not present a very pleasing image of market morality. In his description (which is by no means uniformly hostile), *laissez-faire* reigned supreme and it produced some morally deformed individuals. The only justification for the activities of Wall Street traders may be that ultimately society gained from the workings of a morally unappealing market system. To condemn its high incomes, even if they are necessary for the market to work, and to campaign for their removal, even if that led to lower standards of living, would be an example of the obverse of greed—envy. Even so sceptical (and amusing) a critic as Lewis conceded that the market in the 1980s did work, but 'messily'.[11]

As is well known, even Adam Smith regretted the fact that commercial striving seemed to undermine communal ethics, and indeed the 'martial spirit.' He questioned whether a society driven purely by commerce was sustainable in the long run and he doubted its attractiveness. Still, is it not better that individuals should fight, in a civilised manner, over market share rather than kill each other over bits of land and fragments of ideology?

Wall Street and the Community

A further basis of the argument that Wall Street dealers commit harm is that the reorganisation of industry that their activities produces injures not only identifiable agents but the 'community'. The junk bond dealer might not directly injure someone in an intentional sense (in the way that a criminal does) but the takeovers that his activities finance displace managements, devastate communities and burden the economy with unsustainable debt. As I have said before, these are strictly economic arguments that are susceptible to empirical investigation. However, from a moral perspective, it is highly contentious to attribute 'blame' to individuals for outcomes which they did not intentionally bring about. Some managements will always be displaced in any type of economic reorganisation and failure to guarantee job security is not the same thing as inflicting harm. In the context of economies characterised by change and uncertainty, all that can be said is that in the long run the gainers from reorganisation hypothetically compensate the losers.

This is no doubt unsatisfactory from an ethical perspective since ethics tends to deal with concrete cases of misfortune (which are usually easy to find) whereas political economy is concerned with abstract persons and anonymous processes. It is the former interest that has driven some American states to write statutes regulating takeovers in such a way that 'stakeholders' are protected to the cost of the stockholders (whose right to sell is restricted). But does not this also involve harm in both the narrow and broadened sense? Such legislation attenuates legitimate individual property rights and impedes the competitive process. The legislation ignores the ethical conflict that must exist between different and competing claims to 'rights'.

The Ethics of Regulation

There is, however, another ethical side to governmental regulation of business which is not often considered. This is the ethics of regulation itself; a subject that goes beyond the alleged efficiency-reducing effects of such intervention. For in the hysteria that surrounded scandals in both the City of London and on Wall Street some elementary principles of ethics and the rule of law were overlooked.

There is an important reason why they are likely to be so neglected. It is that regulation of conduct in financial markets tends to go beyond traditional civil and criminal law rules against fraud and deception. Nobody could possibly deny that investors should get the maximum protection against criminal activity (though not against loss) but regulation is normally inspired by 'higher' ideals: values that attempt to implement, for example, more expansive notions of fairness and equality of opportunity than would be sanctioned by arm's length morality. They are predicated on the claim that markets and the traditional legal system do not filter out the greed and arrogance of financial dealers.

The SEC has been decisive in extending dramatically the rules that govern Wall Street: it was instrumental in making insider dealing both a criminal and civil offence, widening its scope to include people not normally thought to be insiders (although the Supreme Court has restrained the SEC in some cases) and the production of a maze of regulations which make life unpredictable for financial operators.[12] It has a kind of roving commission to eliminate what has been ruled as financial misdemeanour. It is apparent that in the investigation by the SEC of Drexel, Burnham, Lambert, the firm did not know what the wrongs were for which it was being questioned. It is this kind of phenomenon which has given rise to the doubts about the compatibility of excessive regulation and the rule of law.

The ideal of the rule of law presupposes that laws should be perfectly general and non-discriminatory, known in advance, comprehensible to all rational agents, predictable in their effects, non-retrospective in their character, and that they should guarantee all suspects a fair and open trial. They are actually strict standards which even most liberal societies can on occasion be excused in not satisfying perfectly.[13] Indeed, the admitted complexity of financial dealings, and the undoubted sophistication of its major players, has licensed, without too much popular disapproval, a certain laxity in the application of strict legal standards in this area. Yet the actions of regulators and prosecuting authorities should be subject to as much ethical scrutiny as the more publicised ones of those agents whom they supervise.

In some respects the investigation of Drexel, Burnham, Lambert and Michael Milken seemed to fall below accepted ethical standards. The first general point is that the SEC, and the US Attorney in New York City, seemed to be responding to public outcry over Wall Street·in their rigorous pursuit of the junk bond personnel. It might be that much wrong was done in the 1980s but the rule of law requires that the wrong be specified and properly adjudicated. The vagueness of some of the charges brought against Milken, and the very fact that the original indictment was reduced to six, suggests that, at the very least, the incidence of regulations cannot be predicted by the affected parties.

There is also a certain investigatory zeal by regulators of financial cases which public opinion inspires, and which is not so apparent in ordinary crime. In the US the Racketeer Influenced and Corrupt Organisations Act (RICO) is used as a kind of threat against suspects by the authorities. RICO is a tough statute (of questionable constitutional validity) which empowers the government to seize assets of suspects before trial. It was originally intended to apply to the Mafia. The threat of a RICO indictment eventually induced Drexel, Burnham, Lambert to settle with the SEC: a costly settlement ($650 million) which effectively ruined the company. It is apparent that RICO was used to induce Milken to make his plea bargain; though the law was never intended for that purpose. There is no doubt that if the kind of legal machinery used in financial cases were to be used in ordinary crime there would be a great outcry from civil rights activists.

Again, the whole notion of plea bargaining sits uneasily with the rule of law doctrine. Undoubtedly, there are efficiency gains to be made from it; the suspect might get off lightly and the state is saved time and money in complex investigatory and legal work. In ordinary crime the suspect probably gains from it but this is less likely in fraud cases. For example, the dropping of insider dealing charges in Milken's case was almost certainly due to the impossibility of sustaining them. Milken was privy to a vast amount of inside information and it is doubtful that he could have hidden from the SEC any misuse of it. But the real point is that no matter how great the efficiency gains are from plea bargaining, it is an affront to strict justice. Although that may be an acceptable cost in a utilitarian-based business ethics, it is unsatisfactory to those who take a more expansive view of the morality of commerce. The latter would include adherents of arm's length morality, since this ethics does include the rule of law as a necessary feature of business life.

A further crucially important feature of plea bargaining is that it has made genuine moral argument about the ethics of Wall Street virtually impossible.

The real tragedy of the Milken case is that, because of the method of its resolution, we will never know what wrongs were done in the financial world of the 1980s. Moral debate will continue to be dominated by emotive accusations and counter-accusations in which a reasoned business ethics will scarcely get a hearing.

In the sentencing of financial miscreants there is a similar moral opacity. There is no settled agreement about the appropriate sentences for crimes. Even though American statute law permits massive prison sentences, these are rarely imposed and judges have considerable discretion. How should this prerogative be used? Both the deterrence principle and the justice principle have been invoked and both could lead to heavy prison sentences. The deterrence principle would be aimed at 'cleaning up' the allegedly sleazy financial world by the threat of heavy punishment irrespective of the intrinsic badness of the particular act. In fact, individuals could be made 'scapegoats' and denied strict justice. The justice principle could still lead to a stiff prison sentence if the offence is adjudged to be particularly heinous. But given that there is a genuine doubt about the moral nature of financial crime, the morality of sentencing remains a contentious matter.

The ten-year prison sentence originally imposed on Milken seemed to be explicable in terms of a combination of deterrence and the need for some expression of public disapproval and perhaps vengeance (a desire fuelled by the fact that Milken would still be a very rich man after he had paid his massive original $600 million fine). Neither rationale seems to have much to do with justice. But the whole problem was made even more confused by the introduction of a bizarre principle by the sentencing judge, Kimba Wood. She said that Milken had 'committed crimes that are hard to detect, *and crimes that are hard to detect warrant greater punishment in order to be effective in deterring others from committing them*'[14] (my italics). I wonder what principles of legal ethics that is meant to exemplify?

An SEC for Britain?

This digression into Milken's case, in addition to being of intrinsic moral importance, has a more general significance for the regulation of securities markets. It is often argued that Britain should have a body like the SEC, with its investigatory powers, in addition to the criminal law and the statutory framework of self-regulation. There is, in Britain, a similar public disapproval of the City of London as there is of Wall Street by American opinion, and a feeling that major crimes go on undetected. Already (1990) a House of Commons Committee has recommended a tightening-up of the law on insider trading.[15] Many critics recommend stiff prison sentences for offenders when apprehended (to date only one person has been given a prison sentence for the offence[16]) and, also, the need for civil suits of the American type in such cases. The introduction of plea bargaining to make convictions easier to secure has also been recommended.

However, in all the major City scandals the normal criminal process has been found to be adequate. The Department of Trade and Industry Inspectors and the Serious Fraud Squad and other bodies perform functions similar to those of the agencies in the US; and trial by jury, despite the scepticism expressed by some observers, clearly still has a crucial role in fraud cases. The Guinness trial showed this; though it has to be conceded that the law involved in that affair was relatively simple. However, in my opinion the introduction of plea bargaining would be to derogate from the rule of law and would probably harm the interests of supects and the public at large.

No doubt there are crimes that go undetected under the present arrangements. But crimes must be distinguished from ethical misconduct. Regulatory bodies that have great investigatory powers and which operate under the auspices of vague statutes tend to confuse ethical misconduct, which should be subject to serious censure, and crime, which should be punished according to strict rules of law. Agencies which are themselves not regulated by strict rules of law, as the SEC appears not to be so regulated, tend to acquire powers which are inimical to freedom and morality. Ethics requires that the regulators may be held up to the same standards as the regulated. The success of the Guinness prosecution suggests that the best way people can be protected in the City is in the rigorous attack on crime by normal police methods. The regulatory bodies established under the Financial Services Act seem not to have been successful in the prevention of wrong-doing; yet they have burdened financial institutions with heavy, and efficiency-reducing, responsibilities.

6 Conclusion

The preceding chapters have been concerned with the ethical problems that confront all business agents, be they stockholders of large corporations, chief executives and others employed in management, small-scale owner-proprietors or even participants in monetary transactions where specific organisational forms are absent. The variety of relationships that these personnel find themselves in generates certain moral questions: How ought I to act under these circumstances? What would be the right price to charge if I were in a position of market 'power'? How much information about this product ought I to reveal? To what extent should the business decision be influenced by the effect it has on unknown people? How much should a not unnatural desire for profit be checked and controlled by widely shared tuistic principles (those that have a regard for other persons)?

The range of questions could be extended almost indefinitely. What differentiates the questions of business ethics from their equivalents in other moral discourse is that the answers to them invariably involve critical reflection on the psychological mainspring of commercial activity, self-interest. The fact that behaviour in exchange economies is powered by it is undeniable; and as long as human beings remain as they are it is probably ineradicable if societies are to progress. Nevertheless, it is a force powerful enough in commerce to repel many people: so much so that they eject the business enterprise from the moral universe. For moral ascetics and Christian theologians it is at most a regrettable necessity, which is capable of moral achievement only when sanitised by abstract principles derived from sources external to it. Contemporary business ethicists of a more secular turn (including many who are not necessarily hostile to commerce and the profit motive) attempt a similar cleansing process when they suggest that business activity should be moralised by principles drawn from moral and political philosophy; as when egalitarianism, social justice, civil liberties doctrines and communal values are applied to the market and to the workplace.

What all these principles of ethical correction have to confront is the problem that if they were applied rigorously to business they would seriously attenuate the mechanisms which drive and galvanise the system. It could be said that they already have. Critics of business who are inspired by some of these principles also neglect, or underplay, the fact that business itself is a moral enterprise. After all, exchange and co-operation between rational and consenting adults, even when it is conducted through the medium of money, are not surely undesirable features of human action. Although Adam Smith lamented the decline of the 'martial spirit' that commercial society produced he still admired the prudence, probity and self-restraint of the businessman. Again, self-interest is not merely the driving force of the 'Invisible Hand' but a means for the achievement of personal autonomy and independence. In his view there was no dichotomy between virtue and commerce as Mandeville had supposed (and which many people mistakenly assume today).

However, what characterises the modern Western world is its openness, pluralism and anonymity: features which have weakened dramatically the hold of those communal, non-individualistic bonds that had traditionally tempered the potential excesses of self-interest. Those face-to-face relationships that perhaps once restrained the desire for self-advancement have been replaced by abstract rules and formal contracts which together govern transient connections between agents who are essentially strangers. Nevertheless, I have suggested that the arm's length morality that is a feature of the modern business world is itself a significant restraining force and contains crucial notions of trust and honesty. It may not be as visible and effective as, say, the Japanese business culture, but when supplemented by the self-correcting mechanisms of the market, a specified set of property rights and a predictable legal order, it can constitute a commercial order that filters out some of the typical ethical problems in business.

Of course on some occasions, the business agent with any sense of morality will specifically *not* treat his customers as total strangers; the producer of potentially unsafe products will make better moral decisions if he imagines them being consumed by a close relative. Still, the Western business community is manifestly not like a family and hence certain artificial constraints on action are all that we have for the production of business morality. The absence of close and informal ties between people means that some of the more extreme demands for a 'socially responsible' business system seem quite inappropriate: the implementation of them would weaken the formal links that we do have, especially those that are governed by property rules. This does not mean that business is socially irresponsible just because it limits itself to the pursuit of profit within the rules of law and conventional morality; and there is nothing in them that prevents supererogatory moral action. Indeed, the last is likely to prosper within a successful commercial order.

Those who recommend that the corporation should refrain from damaging the environment even when permitted by law, or that takeover activity should be curtailed in the interests of a community which is wider than the shareholders, or would introduce 'positive discrimination' in the workplace, often have a difficulty in explaining why these are moral obligations that have a special application to business. The answer often given is that such activity actually 'pays', that 'good' business is indeed good business. But this is something of a paradox, if not a deception. For one school of ethics specifically maintains that an action is moral only if it is performed without the thought of any direct gain that might accrue from it. True moral action, it is said, is motivated by the goodwill itself and not the good consequences of it, either to society or to agents themselves. Such a strict deontology is not entirely absent from the business world: the securities market is, or ought to be, governed by rules whose rationale is justice to the players rather than immediate utility. Arm's length morality itself enjoins a certain kind of crucially important restraint on business agents. Still, it has to be conceded that all of this covers only a small part of business activity.

The cynic might then say that the business moralist who recommends virtue because it pays is not really recommending virtue at all: he has simply found a new and more persuasive (indeed, more marketable) way of profit-seeking. Was Mandeville right after all, then, with his claim that virtue and commerce are antithetical? Has not the modern business moralist simply commercialised virtue? A genuine moral choice should surely involve the possibility of loss?

I think that the Mandevillian dichotomy is too stark. It is still possible to speak of ethics in business: deontology is not the only type of moral philosophy and indeed to follow its prescriptions to the letter would be to render business (or almost any other human activity) impossible. Utilitarianism, the doctrine that good and bad, right and wrong, and so on, are inextricably bound up with beneficial consequences is a strong feature of our moral imagination, especially in our vision of an ideal business world. The moral injunction to act so as to produce the most beneficial consequences interprets these not only as pleasures for individuals but for society as a whole, albeit in a rather incalculable way. Business has then some moral validation in other ways than the immediate satisfactions it brings to its personnel. What makes this a difficult moral achievement is that acts of immediate gratification do not always tend to social happiness or to the long-run interests of each individual utility-maximiser. Business morality has clear public good features and it is this that makes Mandevillianism inadequate because the production of this good requires a certain self-restraint which that eighteenth-century cynic thought impossible.

It is in this context that we can view 'self-regulation' of business in a more favourable light than it normally is. It is actually in the interests (in a utilitarian sense) of individuals and society that government regulation of business be limited. This is because it is often designed at the behest of special interest groups, it is cumbersome, and it coagulates the veins and arteries of commercial society. Also, the morality of politics has no compelling claim to superiority over the morality of business. It is therefore in the long-run interest to practise that restraint on egoism which Mandevillianism assumes to be impossible (or hypocritical). Business organisations are not necessarily conspiracies against the public interest (even Adam Smith had occasionally suggested that they were) but can be viewed as devices to get over the public good problem that inhibits moral action in commerce. The emergence in the securities industry, insurance, accountancy and so on of self-regulatory bodies is to be welcomed; and it would be fallacious to assume that if they are not part of the conventional legal machinery they must be ineffective. It must be remembered that the professions have a direct interest in disciplining their members. The existence of these bodies is quite consistent with arm's length morality. That these movements have not been as successful as many had hoped (see, for example, Arrow's case for them outlined in Chapter 1) is perhaps a commentary on the all-pervading presence of 'Prisoner's Dilemmas' in society rather than the special venality of businessmen.

These kinds of problems are no better illustrated than in the question of the environment,[1] which is likely to be the major issue for business for the foreseeable future. For although each business agent may view the earth as a common and free good to be exploited without restraint, the sum of their activities produce bad outcomes for everybody. Pollution is not necessarily bad, it is the *extra* bit that causes the problem and since the person creating this cannot be identified, the business community as a whole is condemned. Since future generations are the victims of the present generation's desire for immediate gratification, the virtue of business as a complex web of relationships between strangers is stretched to the limit.

Arm's length morality has its most vociferous critics here but it cannot be said that communitarian business cultures fare any better. There is no evidence that the Japanese business world, with its apparent anti-individualistic bias, has produced a more pleasing environment or that its much-vaunted concern for the preservation of an existing culture has produced a more generous attitude towards the inheritors of that culture. Again, although the profit-maximising corporation is blamed for all environmental ills, socialist societies have, by common scientific agreement,[2] and casual observation, produced ecological nightmares. The state in Eastern Europe has shown scant regard for the present and future generations in its relentless exploitation of natural resources. The now well-documented environmental catastrophes in former communist countries have been achieved without the intrusion of the profit motive.

The reason why capitalist societies, even in the least propitious circumstances, actually have better environmental records that their rivals is precisely because arm's length morality is conducted in a world of self-correcting mechanisms.[3] One of these is the law. At least in commercial societies there is the possibility of suing violators and although the inadequate specification of property rights makes this difficult, one should not dismiss this approach. It is at least in principle capable of improvement. In socialist societies environmental damage proceeds apace precisely because there is no possibility of suing the state.

Again, the market performs important corrective functions. People do not like living in a badly polluted environment and punish corporations which violate their rights as citizens. It is often forgotten that a concern for their environment is a feature of rich societies (which are largely the creation of a capitalist development) and their inhabitants are beginning to treat clean air, green fields, and so on as wanted goods for which they are prepared to pay a high price. Since much of corporate investment is controlled by financial institutions, significant pressure can be brought to bear on recalcitrant managements. In the US all major corporations are taking steps to respond to this pressure.[4] This is not just a cynical response by business to the threat of even more restrictive legislation but an attempt to satisfy the wants of their customers. People are beginning to recognise that to rely solely on legislation in this area is potentially dangerous. Legislation over the environment tends to be promoted by enthusiasts who would protect the environment at any cost. To do this is to ignore the delicate trade-offs between productivity and environmental protection that a free society has to make.

It is true that minimal legal rules and corrective market mechanisms are not enough. There are genuine public good problems in this area. The temptation of business agents to despoil the environment, and indeed cause harm to unknown persons, may be irresistible precisely because of the short-run, profit-maximising imperative that governs their actions. However, the argument should not be presented as a battle between business and the environment. A reliance solely on the finality of legislation, prohibition rather than adjustment, is likely to be as harmful to the interests of anonymous members of the public as a dependence on self-correcting mechanisms alone.

These are only preliminary observations in what is clearly a large and crucially important topic. I make them only to suggest that there is a use even in superficially unpromising areas for the much-derided business morality of Western capitalism.

Notes

Chapter 1 pp. 1 to 24
1. Quoted in R Reidenbach and D P Robin, *Ethics and Profits*, Englewood Cliffs, New Jersey, Prentice Hall, 1989.
2. See Reidenbach and Robin, op cit, ch 1.
3. R DeGeorge, *Business Ethics*, New York, Macmillan, 1982, ch 8.
4. J K Galbraith, *The New Industrial State*, Harmondsworth, Penguin, 1974
5. See R Nader, M Green and J Seligman, *Taming the Corporate Giant*, New York, W W Norton, 1976.
6. See M Friedman's 'The Social Responsibility of Business is to Increase Its Profits'. Reprinted in T Beauchamp and N Bowie (eds), *Ethical Theory and Business*, Englewood Cliffs, New Jersey, Prentice Hall, 1988. First published 1970.
7. F B Kaye (ed), Oxford, Clarendon Press, 1924. First published 1705.
8. Friedman, op.cit. p 87.
9. See A Hirschman, 'Rival Interpretations of Market Society', *Journal of Economic Literature*, XX 1982, pp 1463–1484.
10. See Michael Novak, *Towards A Theology of the Corporation*, Washington, American Enterprise Institute, 1981.
11. 'Social Responsibility and Economic Efficiency', in W Shaw and V Barry, *Moral Issues in Business*, Belmont, California, Wadsworth Publishing Company, 1989, pp 213–18.
12. See P Pettit, 'The Prisoner's Dilemma and Social Theory', *Politics*, 1985.
13. See F A Hayek, *The Mirage of Social Justice*, London, Routledge and Kegan Paul, 1976.
14. For a critique of market socialism, see D Lavoie, *Rivalry or Central Plan?*, Cambridge, Cambridge University Press, 1985.
15. See DeGeorge, op cit, chs 2, 3, 4. and 5.
16. See A Quinton, *Utilitarianism*, London, Oxford University Press, 1978.
17. For a description and critique of Paretian welfare economics, see C K Rowley and A T Peacock, *Welfare Economics : A Liberal Restatement*, London, Martin Robertson, 1975, Part One.
18. See M Snoeyenbos, R Almeder and J Humber, 'Cost Benefit Analysis and the Ford Pinto', in Snoeyenbos, Almeder and Humber (eds), *Business Ethics*, New York, Prometheus Books, 1983, pp 69–72.
19. See Reidenbach and Robin, op cit, pp 133–6.
20. DeGeorge, op cit, pp 43–7.
21. Ibid, op cit, pp 58–63.

22. *The Theory of Moral Sentiments*, E West (ed), Indianapolis, Liberty Classics, 1969, p 160. First published 1759.
23. F A Hayek, *The Mirage of Social Justice*, London, Routledge and Kegan Paul, 1976.
24. R Nozick, *Anarchy, State and Utopia*, Oxford, Blackwell, 1974, ch 8.
25. See DeGeorge, op cit, pp 113–19.
26. K Haakonssen, *The Science of a Legislator*, Cambridge, Cambridge University Press, 1981.
27. 'Selling the Lockheed Tristar' in Snoeyenbos, Almeder and Humber, op cit, pp 138–44.
28. See G Becker, *The Economic Approach to Human Behaviour*, Chicago, University of Chicago Press, 1976.
29. R Soloman and K Hansen, *It's Good Business*, New York, Atheneum, 1985, p 36.
30. See I Kirzner, *Discovery, Capitalism, and Distributive Justice*, Oxford, Blackwell, 1989.
31. A Etzioni, *The Moral Dimension*, New York, Free Press, 1988.

Chapter Two pp. 25 to 48

1. 'It is not from the benevolence of the butcher, the brewer or the baker that we expect our dinner, but from their regard to their own interest.' Adam Smith, *The Wealth of Nations*, R H Campbell and A S Skinner (eds), Oxford, Clarendon Press, 1970, pp 26–7. First published in 1776.
2. Ibid, vol I, Book 11, ch 8.
3. Ibid, pp 740–58.
4. A Berle and G Means, *The Modern Corporation and Private Property*, New York, Harcourt, Brace and World, revised edition, 1967, p 116. For a theory of modern business organisation, see M Ricketts, *The Economics of Business Enterprise*, Brighton, Wheatsheaf, 1987.
5. Galbraith, op cit.
6. Nader, op cit. For a critique of Nader, see R Hessen, *In Defence of the Corporation*, Stanford, Hoover Institution Press, 1979.
7. D Reisman, *Galbraith and Market Capitalism*, London, Macmillan, 1980.
8. Ricketts, op cit, ch 1.
9. See I Kirzner, *Competition and Entrepreneurship*, Chicago, University of Chicago Press, 1973.
10. See W Shaw and V Barry, op cit ch 5.
11. R Pilon, 'Corporations and Rights', *Georgia Law Review*, 1979, pp 1246–364.
12. *Capitalism and Freedom*, Chicago, University of Chicago Press, 1962.
13. 'The Social Responsibility of Business is to Increase Its Profits', in Beauchamp and Bowie, op cit, p 87.
14. *The Modern Corporation and Social Responsibility*, Washington, American Enterprise Institute, 1972, p 29.
15. This happened, for example, over South African investment.
16. See Michael Keeley, *A Social-Contract Theory of Organizations*, Notre Dame, University of Notre Dame Press, 1988.
17. See Hessen, *In Defence of the Corporation*, op cit ch 1.
18. W Evan and R Freeman, 'A Stakeholder Theory of the Modern Corporation', in Beauchamp and Bowie, op cit, pp 97–106.
19. *The Theory of Moral Sentiments*, op cit, pp 232–60.

20. See T Donaldson and P Werhane *Ethical Issues in Business*, Englewood Cliffs, Prentice Hall, 1983.
21. Reidenbach and Robin, op cit, pp 27–30.
22. Ibid, p 28.
23. Ibid, pp 133–6.
24. Ibid pp. 46–8.
25. P French, *Corporations and Corporate Responsibility*, New York, Columbia University Press, 1984.
26. Reidenbach and Robin, op cit, pp 44–6.
27. P French, op. cit., pp. 12–16.
28. 'Avoidable Human Errors Afloat and Ashore', *The Times*, 20 October 1990.

Chapter Three pp. 49 to 62

1. The Rawlsian criterion for a just distribution permits inequalities only if they are to the benefit of the least-advantaged. See J Rawls, *A Theory of Justice*, London, Oxford University Press, 1972.
2. D Frantz, *Levine and Co*, New York, Henry Holt, 1987.
3. L Herzel and L Katz, 'Insider Trading: Who Loses?', *Lloyds Bank Review*, 1987 (No 165), p 19.
4. Ibid, pp 19–23.
5. See B Brennan and N Kubasek, *The Legal Environment of Business*, New York, Macmillan, 1988, ch 10.
6. See N Wolfson, 'Civil Liberties and Regulation of Insider Trading', in J Dorn and H Manne (eds), *Economic Liberties and the Constitution*, Fairfax, George Mason University Press, 1987, pp 329–34.
7. B Chiplin and M Wright, *The Logic of Mergers*, London, Institute of Economic Affairs, 1987.
8. H Manne, *Insider Trading and the Stock Market*, New York, Free Press, 1966.
9. Ibid, op cit, p 8.
10. See H Manne, 'Insider Trading and the Law Professors', *Vanderbilt Law Review*, 1970 (23), pp 547–90.
11. H Manne, 'Insider Trading and Property Rights in New Information', in Dorn and Manne, op cit, p 326.
12. Ibid, p 322.
13. D Frantz, op cit, ch 9.
14. Gary Lawson, 'The Ethics of Insider Trading', in *Harvard Journal of Law and Public Policy*, 1988, (11), p 767.
15. H Manne, *Insider Trading and the Stock Market*, op cit, pp 114–39.
16. H Manne 'Insider Trading and the Law Professors', op cit, p 548.
17. I Kirzner, *Discovery, Capitalism and Distributive Justice*, op cit.
18. V Brudney, 'Insiders, Outsiders and Informational Advantages Under the Federal Securities Laws', *Harvard Law Review*, 1979 (93), pp 322–76.
19. See Nozick, *Anarchy, State and Utopia*, op cit.
20. I. Kirzner, *Discovery, Capitalism and Distributive Justice*, op cit, ch 1.

Chapter Four pp. 63 to 73

1. B Chiplin and M Wright, op cit, pp 39–42.
2. Ibid.
3. C Fildes, 'The Importance of Being Honest', *Spectator* 1 September, 1990.

4. J Gulliver, 'How Scotland Lost Out to Hammersmith Flyover', *The Times*, 31 August 1990.
5. M Ricketts, 'Kirzner's theory of Entrepreneurship: A Critique', in S Boehm and B Caldwell, *Austrian Econonmics: Tensions and New Directions*. Forthcoming.
6. Chiplin and Wright, op cit, pp 22–7.
7. Masahiko Aoki, *Information, Incentives and Bargaining in the Japanese Economy*, Cambridge, Cambridge University Press, 1988.
8. See F A Hayek, 'The Principles of a Liberal Social Order', in *Studies in Philosophy, Politics and Economics*, London, Routledge and Kegan Paul, 1967, pp 162–79.
9. Ibid, p 173.
10. W Evans and R Freeman, 'A Stakeholder Theory of the Corporation', in Beauchamp and Bowie, op cit.
11. The best example of this is the Rowntree case. See S Gray and M McDermott, *Mega-Merger Mania*, London, Mandarin, 1990, pp 143–55.
12. Ibid, ch 2.
13. See Chiplin and Wright, op cit, pp 47–50.

Chapter Five pp. 74 to 87

1. Brett Fromsom, 'The Last Days of Drexel Burnham', *Fortune*, May 1990.
2. L P Cohen, 'How Michael Milken Was Forced to Accept the Prospect of Guilt', *Wall Street Journal*, 23 April 1990.
3. For details of Milken's offences, and the text of his own confession, see *Wall Street Journal*, 25 April 1990.
4. See L Gordon Crovitz, 'Milken Prosecution: The Rise and Fall of Allegations', *Wall Street Journal*, 27 February 1991. For an iconoclastic and clever argument that Milken was a victim of a modern version of the offence of witchcraft, see Pierre Lemieux, *Apologie des Sorcières Modernes*, Paris, Les Belles Lettres, 1991.
5. See L Gordon Crovitz, 'Milken and His Enemies', *National Review*, October 1990.
6. See Amar Chide, 'In Praise of Corporate Raiders', *Policy Review*, pp 21–4.
7. L P Cohen, 'Milken's Stiff Ten Year Sentence', *Wall Street Journal*, 25 November 1990.
8. See L Gordon Crovitz, 'Punish Milken for what He Did, Not what Prosecutors Say He Did', *Wall Street Journal*, 26 September 1990; also Crovitz, 'Milken Punishment Fits No Crime He Committed', *Wall Street Journal*, 28 November 1990.
9. New York, Penguin, 1988.
10. New York, Penguin, 1989.
11. Letters Page, *The Wall Street Journal*, 23 May 1991.
12. See L Gordon Crovitz, 'The SEC Overstepped the Mark When It Made Insider Trading a Crime', *Wall Street Journal*, 19 December 1990.
13. See F A Hayek, *The Constitution of Liberty*, London, Routledge and Kegan Paul, 1960, ch 15.
14. Quoted in Cohen, 'Milken's Stiff Ten Year Sentence' op cit.
15. G Serjeant, 'Committee Calls for Overhaul of Insider Law' *The Times*, 24 May 1990.
16. Ivor Goodman received eighteen months jail, see *Daily Telegraph*, 1 May 1991. See also, Brenda Hannigan, *Insider Dealing*, London Kluwer, 1988.

Chapter Six pp. 88 to 92

1. See D Pearce, A Markandya, and B Barbia, *Blueprint for a Green Economy*, London, Earthscan Publications, 1989.
2. See W K Reilly, 'The Green Thumb of Capitalism', *Policy Review*, Fall, 1990, pp 16–21.
3. See R Stroup, 'The Market: Conservation's Best Friend', *Wall Street Journal*, 19 April 1990; M Bernstam, *The Wealth of Nations and the Environment*, London, Institute of Economic Affairs, 1991.
4. D Kirkpatrick, 'Environmentalism: the New Crusade', *Fortune*, February 1990.

The David Hume Institute

The David Hume Institute was registered in January 1985 as a company limited by guarantee: its registration number in Scotland is 91239. It is recognised as a Charity by the Inland Revenue.

The objects of the Institute are to promote discourse and research on economic and legal aspects of public policy questions. It has no political affiliations.

The Institute regularly publishes two series of papers. In the **Hume Paper** series, published by Aberdeen University Press, the results of original research by commissioned authors are presented in plain language. **The Hume Occasional Paper** series presents shorter pieces by members of the Institute, by those who have lectured to it and by those who have contributed to 'in-house' research projects. From time to time, important papers which might otherwise become generally inaccessible are presented in the **Hume Reprint Series**. A complete list of the Institute's publications follows.

Hume Papers

Published by Aberdeen University Press

17 Beyond the Welfare State: An Examination of Basic Incomes in a Market Economy *Samuel Brittan*

Hume Occasional Papers
No.1 What to Do About the Over-Valued Dollar *Ronald McKinnon*
No.2 The Political Economy of Pension Provision *Alan Peacock* and *Norman Barry*
No.3 The Regularities of Regulation *George J Stigler*
No.4 How Safe is the Banking System? *Richard Dale*
No.5 Economic Issues in Merger Policy (Out of print) *E Victor Morgan*
No.6 The Regulation of the Telecommunications Industry *Bryan Carsberg*
No.7 The Novelist's View of the Market Economy *Allan Massie*
No.8 Understanding Mrs Thatcher: Conservative Economic Policy 1979–1987 *David Simpson*
No.9 Adam Smith and Economic Liberalism *Andrew Skinner*
No.10 Long-term Savings in an Enterprise Economy: A Case Study of the Principles and Practice of UK Economic Policy *Jack Wiseman*
No.11 Contemporary Problems in Commerical Litigation *David Edward, Lord Ross with a Commentary by Catherine Montgomery Blight*
No.12 Industry, Money and Markets: A Means to Irish Unification *W Duncan Reekie*
No.13 The Future of Legal Systems *Thijmen Koopmans*
No.14 Mergers and Takeovers: Short and Long-Term Issues *Sir Gerald Elliot*
No.15 The Takeover Boom: An International and Historical Perspective *Graham Bannock*
No.16 The Regulation of the Water Industry. The Office of Water Services: Structure & Policy *Ian Byatt*
No.17 Corporate Takeovers and the Interests of Regions and Local Communities *Brian Ashcroft* and *James H Love*
No.18 Evidence Submitted to the Inquiry into Corporate Takeovers in the United Kingdom, Vol 1
No.19 Takeover Activity and Differential Returns to Shareholders of Bidding Companies *Robin Limmack*
No.20 Finance and Takeovers *David Gowland*
No.21 The UK Panel on Takeovers and Mergers: An Appraisal *W A P Manser*
No.22 Corporate Takeovers—The Need for Fundamental Rethinking *Allen Sykes*
No.23 The Stock Market and Mergers in the United Kingdom *E Victor Morgan* and *Ann D Morgan*

Books
The Deregulation of Financial Markets
edited by Richard Dale, Woodhead-Faulkner, London, 1986
Governments and Small Business
Graham Bannock and Alan Peacock, Paul Chapman, London, 1989

Hume Reprints
No.1 The 'Politics' of Investigating Broadcasting Finance *Alan Peacock*
No.2 Spontaneous Order and the Rule of Law *Neil MacCormick*

Hume Papers No. 8 et seq. may be obtained from Aberdeen University Press, Farmers Hall, Aberdeen AB9 2XT, Scotland, Tel 0224 641672.
Other publications may be obtained from The Secretary, The David Hume Institute, 21 George Square, Edinburgh EH8 9LD, Tel 031 667 7004: Fax 031 667 9111.